A-Z BURTON UPON TRENT

GW01451622

CONTENTS

Key to Map Pages	2-3
Map Pages	4-41

Inde
Villa
and

REFERENCE

A Road	**A38**
B Road	**B5008**
Dual Carriageway	
One-way Street	→
Traffic flow on A Roads is also indicated by a heavy line on the driver's left.	→
Road Under Construction	
Opening dates are correct at the time of publication.	
Proposed Road	
Restricted Access	
Pedestrianized Road	
Track	
Footpath	
Residential Walkway	
Railway Level Crossing Station	✦
Built-up Area	DERBY STREET
Local Authority Boundary	— ·· — ·· —
Posttown Boundary	
Postcode Boundary	
(within posttown)	
Map Continuation	19

Car Park (selected)	🅿
Church or Chapel	†
Fire Station	■
Hospital	⊞
House Numbers (A & B Roads only)	61 19
Information Centre	🛈
National Grid Reference	320
Police Station	▲
Post Office	★
Safety Camera with Speed Limit	30
Fixed cameras and long term road works cameras. Symbols do not indicate camera direction.	
Toilet: without facilities for the Disabled	▽
with facilities for the Disabled	▽
Disabled use only	▽
Educational Establishment	
Hospital or Healthcare building	
Industrial Building	
Leisure or Recreational Facility	
Place of Interest	
Public Building	
Shopping Centre or Market	
Other Selected Buildings	

SCALE

1:19,000

0	¼	½	¾ Mile
0 250 500 750 Metres 1 Kilometre			

3⅓ inches (8.47 cm) to 1 mile
5.26 cm to 1 kilometre

Copyright of Geographers' A-Z Map Company Limited

Fairfield Road, Borough Green, Sevenoaks, Kent TN15 8PP
Telephone: 01732 781000 (Enquiries & Trade Sales)
          01732 783422 (Retail Sales)

www.az.co.uk
Copyright © Geographers' A-Z Map Co. Ltd.
Edition 4   2013

Ordnance Survey® This product includes mapping data licensed from Ordnance Survey® with the permission of the Controller of Her Majesty's Stationery Office.

2

B5030
A50
A515
B5027
A518
B5013
B5017
Uttoxeter
River Dove
A50
A515
B5017

Etwall

Hatton
4
Hilton
5
6

Marston
on Dove
Tutbury

Rolleston
on Dove
Egginton

8
9
Stretton
10

Horninglow
Anslow
Newton
Solney

Abbots Bromley
B5234
Outwoods

Winshill

Blithfield
Reservoir
B5234

12
13
14

BURTON UPON TRENT

A515
River Trent
B5014

Tatenhill
Stapenhill

Branston

Inset Page 16
Yoxall

16
17
18
19
20

Barton-under-Needwood
Walton-on-Trent
Castle Gresley

A513
Efflinch
Caldwell
Linton

A513
Rosliston

24
25
26
27
28

Handsacre
B5014
A51
A515
Alrewas
Coton in the Elms

Trent & Mersey Canal
A513
A38
A513

River Tame
River Mease

A5192

LICHFIELD
A5127

A5199
A38
B5495
A51

SCALE

0	1	2	3 Miles
0	1	2	3	4 Kilometres

DERBY

Long Eaton

A52 · A516 · A5250 · A5111 · A514 · A52 · A514 · B5010 · B5020 · A6 · A6005 · A52 · B6540 · 25

A516 · A38

Findern

7

Willington

Chellaston

A50 · A5132 · A514 · B587 · B5010 · River Derwent · Trent & Mersey Canal · River Trent

A50 · 24a · A453 · A6 · 24

Repton

11

Inset Page 11

Castle Donington

EAST MIDLANDS ✈

A453 · DONNINGTON PARK · S · 23a · A42 · Brook · Westmeadow

15

Bretby

Foremarks Reservoir

B5006 · A514

Staunton Harold Reservoir

B5324 · M1

Newhall

Lower Midway

Hartshorne

Belton

Shepshed

21 · 22 · 23

Smisby

SWADLINCOTE

Blackfordby

A511 · B587 · A42 · B5324 · A512 · 23

ASHBY-DE-LA-ZOUCH

Coleorton

Thringstone

Swannington

29 · 30 · 31 · 32 · 33 · 34 · 35

verseal

Norris Hill

Moira

Packington

Sinope

Whitwick

Donisthorpe

Ravenstone

Agar Nook

COALVILLE

Oakthorpe

Normanton le Heath

36 · 37 · 38 · 39 · 40 · 41

Measham

Swepstone

Heather

Ellistown

Bardon Hill

A444 · A511 · A50 · 22 · S · B591

LEICESTER (MARKFIELD)

11

Ibstock

Inset Page 40

Appleby Magna

Snarestone

M42 · A444 · B4116 · B5493 · B582 · B585 · A447 · B585 · M1

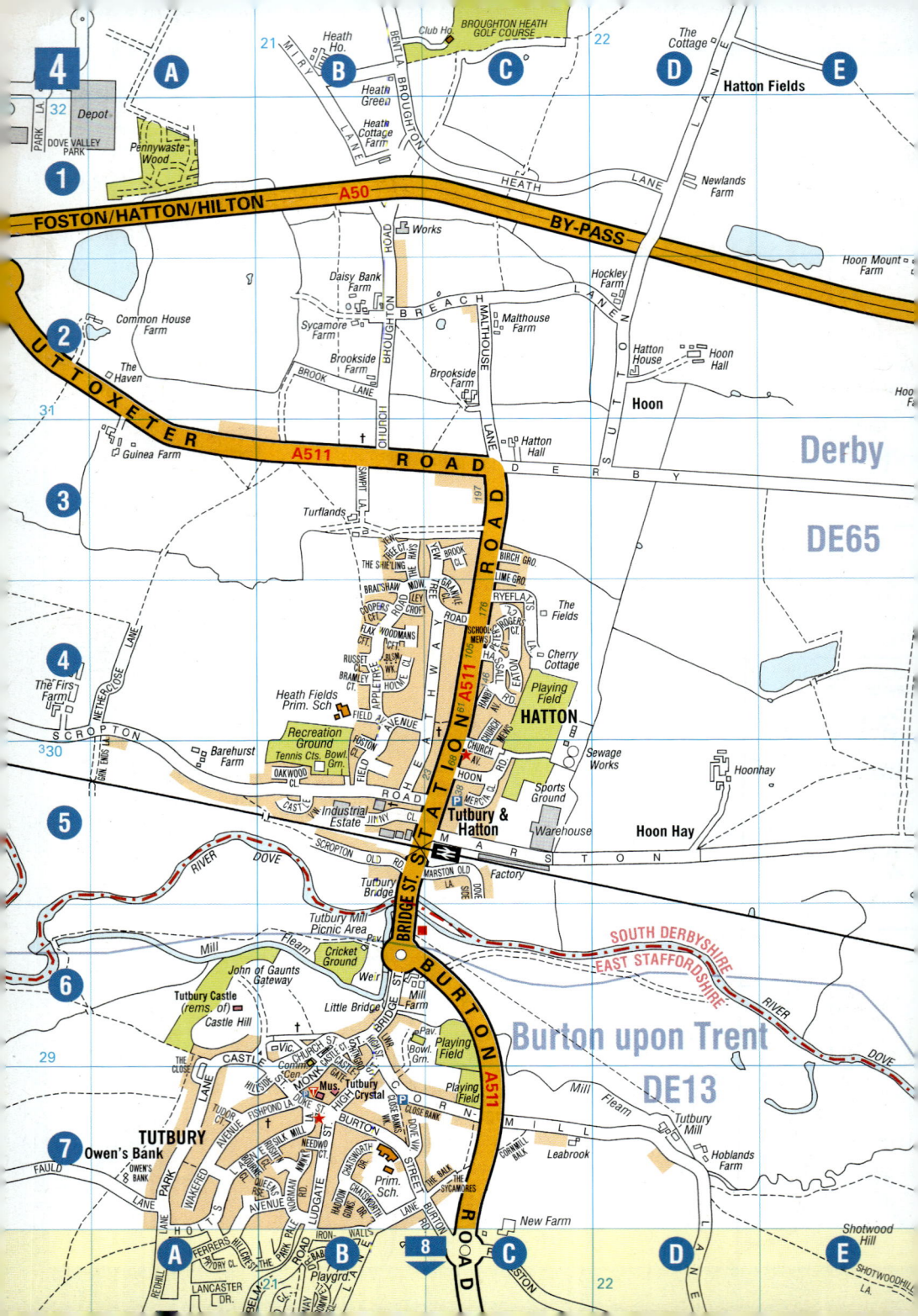

4

A B C D E

21 22

Heath Ho.

Club Ho.

BROUGHTON HEATH GOLF COURSE

The Cottage

Hatton Fields

32 Depot

PARK LA.

DOVE VALLEY PARK

Pennywaste Wood

Heath Green

Heath Cottage Farm

BENT LA.

BROUGHTON LANE

MIRY LANE

Newlands Farm

1

FOSTON/HATTON/HILTON A50 **BY-PASS**

HEATH LANE

Hoon Mount Farm

Works

Daisy Bank Farm

Sycamore Farm

Brookside Farm

ROAD

BROUGHTON LANE

BREACH LANE

Malthouse Farm

Hockley Lane

SUTTON LANE

Hatton House

Hoon Hall

Hoo

Common House Farm

The Haven

2

UTTOXETER

31

Guinea Farm

BROOK LANE

Brookside Farm

MALTHOUSE LANE

Hatton Hall

Hoon

A511 **ROAD**

DERBY

Derby

Turflands

SWEPT LA.

197

DE65

3

The Shieling

BROOK

BIRCH GRO.

LIME GRO.

The Fields

BRADSHAW CL.

COOPERS CFT.

FLAX CFT.

RUSSET CFT.

BRAMLEY CT.

APPLETREE

MOW LEY

YEW TREE

GRANGE

CLOSE

HATHERN CT.

ROGERS CT.

EATON CL.

RYEFLATS

School Mews

Cherry Cottage

Playing Field

HATTON

NETHERCLOSE LANE

The Firs Farm

SCROPTON

330

Barehurst Farm

GIN ENG'S LA.

Heath Fields Prim. Sch.

Recreation Ground

Tennis Cts. Bowl. Grn.

FOSTON CL.

OAKWOOD CL.

FIELD AVENUE

FIELD

ROAD

A511 **STATION**

HANBURY RD.

AVONDALE RD.

CHURCH AV.

HOON RD.

MERCIA

Sports Ground

Sewage Works

Hoonhay

4

CASTLE

Industrial Estate

JINNY CL.

Tutbury & Hatton

Warehouse

Hoon Hay

RIVER DOVE

SCROPTON OLD RD.

MARSTON OLD LA.

DOVE SIDE

Factory

M A R S T O N

5

Tutbury Bridge

Tutbury Mill Picnic Area

Fleam

Mill

Cricket Ground

Weir

Pav.

BRIDGE ST.

RIVER DOVE

6

John of Gaunts Gateway

Tutbury Castle (rems. of)

Castle Hill

Little Bridge

Mill Farm

Pav. Bowl. Grn.

Playing Field

MONK ST.

BRIDGE ST.

MOAT DR.

Burton upon Trent

RIVER DOVE

29

THE CLOSE

CASTLE LANE

HILLSIDE

Vic.

CHURCH ST.

CASTLE ST.

MONK GATE

High St.

Mus. Tutbury Crystal

Playing Field

GATE

CORN CL. RINGS

CLOSE BANK

CORNMILL VALE

Mill

Fleam

Tutbury Mill

DE13

7 Owen's Bank

TUTBURY

FAULD

OWEN'S BANK

PARK LANE

WAKEFIELD

TUDOR CFT.

AVENUE

QUEENS AVENUE

NORMAN RD.

LUDGATE

FISHPOND LA.

DUKE ST.

ASH LE.

BELK MILL

CHATSWORTH CT.

HADDON GDNS.

CHATSWORTH

BURTON STREET

NEEDWOOD ST.

THE BALK

Prim. Sch.

THE SYCAMORES

Hoblands Farm

Leabrook

New Farm

BURTON A511 ROAD

Shotwood Hill

8

A B C D E

REDHILL

FERRERS LA.

HILLCREST

PRIORY CL.

THE FOLD

WALLS

Playgrd.

FOSTON

SHOTWOODHILL LA.

LANCASTER DR.

BELMONT

21 22

SOUTH DERBYSHIRE

EAST STAFFORDSHIRE

F
G
H
J
K
24
425
32
31
330
29
1
2
3
4
5
6
7
Hoon Mount
HOON RIDGE
The Cottage
Hoon Ridge
HOON LANE
SUTTON BROOK
Hilton Gorse
SUTTON LANE
Crotthall Cott.
Burntheath
Blakelow Farm
Rifle Range
WILLOW PIT LANE
Roystone Ho.
A50
FOSTON/HATTON/HILTON
BY-PASS
Works
Junction 5
DERBY RD.
136
A5132
EGGINTON RD.
LUCAS LANE
Elm Tree Farm
Hargate Lodge
9
Hallcroft
DALE END LA.
Grange Farm
Weir
Moorend
Offices
MAIN STREET
ROAD
Sports Ground
Pav.
DERBY ROAD
EGGINTON ROAD
SUTTON LA.
CHERRY TREE CL.
SHADY GROVE
WEST AV.
PERCY WOOD CL.
HILTON
Playing Field
Prim. Sch.
BACK LANE
FIELD CLOSE
PEACROFT CL.
PEACROFT LA.
BANCROFT CL.
HAWTHORN CL.
NEW ROAD
WILLOWFIELDS
NORMANDY RD.
UTAH
SHAEF CL.
BREN WAY
RODNEY CL.
SHERMAN CL.
ENFIELD CL.
MULBERRY WY.
HUNTSPILL RD.
FOSS RD.
FOSS WAY
WINDERMERE DR.
MERSEY WY.
NOTTINGHILL RD.
ISIS WY.
ORWELL RD.
DEE CLOSE
HUMBER
BROOK ST.
WELLAND
THAMES WAY
SOAR CL.
CALDER CL.
AVON WAY
TRUSLEY BROOK
WELLAND RD.
SANDFORD BROOK
BENTLEY BROOK
TINSELL BROOK
MEASE
THE MEASE
WASHFORD
HILTON BUSINESS PARK
HARRISON COURT
LOWMAN WAY
Depot
Sewage Wks.
LYNMOUTH HO.
RICHMOND HO.
BUCKINGHAM HO.
EDEN CL.
Playgrd.
RIBBLE CL.
SEVERN DR.
KYLE RD.
The New Cottages
Brookside
The Grange
Ivy Cottage
Ivy House Farm
Vicarage
LANE
Marston on Dove
The Hall
MARSTON LANE
Dove Bank Farm
HILTON BROOK
Marston Crossing
Dove Bridge
Mill Fleam
OLD RIVER DOVE
RIVER DOVE
Mill Fleam

6

A B C D E

26 27

32

1 Roystone House

ASH LA SUTTON BY-PASS Playing Field Pav LANE BURNASTON LANE LAWNSWOOD

ETWALL BY-PASS Etwall Leisure Centre ALMS-HOUSES ST PORTHILL STREET BLENHEIM M. SLADE CL. SANDYPITS Sandypits Farm The Old Lodge Nursing Home

A516 DERBY ROAD DERBY ROAD HILTON Tennis Courts John Port School Lib PEAR TREE CT. OAKLANDS JOHN PORT CL. LODGE CL. Etwall Lodge ETWALL

Friary Farm Bank Ho. MITCHELLS OLD STATION CL. MEADOW WY. SHIELD WAY BANCROFT King George's Field Etwall Prim. Sch. GERARD SYCAMORE Lodge Farm Rockingham House

STATION RW. THE HILL BLAKE DR. BANCROFT CHESTNUT GROVE BELFIELD BEECH LABURNUM New Acres New Close Cottages

2 Junction 5 DERBY D A50 E R B Y ROAD BELFIELD CT. BELFIELD TER. SPRINGFD Hayes Croft Etwall Hayes Quarnette Highfields

31 Sewage Works COMMON END EGGINTON RD. SPRINGFD RD. GROVE JACKSONS LANE S O U T H Broomhill Cottages

3 Elm Tree Farm TYNEFIELD MEWS TYNEFIELD COURT

Hargate Lodge LUCAS BREN HFX WINN HLFX NG ED EGGINTON Hargate House Farm Blakeley Lodge

4 Hargate Manor A5132 Hargate Fields Farm OLDFIELD LANE Egginton Common Derby DE65 ETWALL COMMON

330 HARRISON COURT WAY LOWMAN Gravelpit Houses B O U N D A R Y

5 HILTON BUSINESS PARK Birch-Trees Farm Dairy Egginton Gorse Gorse Farm Old Station Cottages EGGINTON COMMON

Sewage Wks. ROAD HILTON Hilton Crossing Hinkinhill Park Hill Cottages RAILWAY COTTAGES

6 Egginton Junction The Purbeck Station Farm Park Hill Park View EGGINTON COMMON South Boundary Cottages Gravelpit Plantation

Weir Saltersford Bridge Pump Ho. ROAD CARRIERS Marlpit Plantation A5132 ROAD

29 BLACKSMITHS EGGINTON ROAD ASH GROVE GROVE LANE BRUNT'S

7 HILTON Oaktree Farm Egginton Bridge Ash Grove STREET WILLIAM STREET (Roman)

BROOK Egginton DUCK Manor Fm. Peartree Farm Whitehouse Farm Grange BROOK LANE

A B **10** C D E
26 FISHPOND 27

Burnaston

F G H J K

28 29 430

Manor Cottage

Hill Farm

New Buildings Farm

32

1

MAIN ST.

MILLWAY LA.

GREEN LANE

FINDERN

New Gorse Fox Covert

Depot

Burton

Fields Farm

DOLES

2

Marlpit Plantation

Park House

Nursery

Roseglade

Little Derby House

BARN CL.

Wallfield House

31

3

Coneygree Farm

CAR FACTORY

Four Ways

Highfield

LITTLE DERBY LANE

A38

Tower House

Mill Farm

WEST E.LA.

HILLSIDE

PORTERS

FINDERN

SIDE

AUSTEN

ROAD

AULTS

THRUSTON CL.

THE HAYES

CLOVERS LADE

WREN PARK CL.

MILL CL.

MILL HILL

TOWNSEND

VARSITY

TEST TRACK

Avenue Lodge

Highfield House

ALDERSLEY CL.

CL.

LANE

Longlands Cottage

The Longlands

4

E A50 R N

Fox Covert

TOYOTA ISLAND

Junction 4

BYPASS

A50

Longlands Plantation

LONGLANDS

330

Standpipe Cottages

Round House

Danes Lodge

ETWALL

Derby with Burton Service Area

HEATH LA.

ROAD

5

BURTON ROAD

(Willington) Lane

Hill Farm

Common Plantation

WILLINGTON LANE

Everglades

Trent & Mersey Canal

29

6

Works

B5008

Mercia Marina

ROAD

The Bungalow

Nursery

A38

CANAL BRIDGE

DERWENT AV.

ROAD

Dale Farm

Cemetery

FINDERN

7

214

WATER SIDE

WILLOW GRO.

GREEN LA.

THE GRN.

CHAPEL

ORCHARD CL.

Spts. Grd.

WILLINGTON

THE POTLOCKS

FERN CL.

FERN CL.

WILLINGTON RD.

CASTLE WAY

F G H 11 J K

48 68 TWYFORD A5132 ROAD

105

Willington

THE GREEN Hall

REPTON R.

IVY

SAXON GRO.

TRIM

BELL

OAKS

MERCIA DR.

ST. MICHAEL'S

CROSBY

MARKHAM CT.

CHAPEL ST.

CAMDEN

AVENUE

HALL DR.

LANE

TRENT AV.

SEALEY

JAMES ST.

CLOSE

WHEATHOFT CL.

139

129 128

30

29

Green

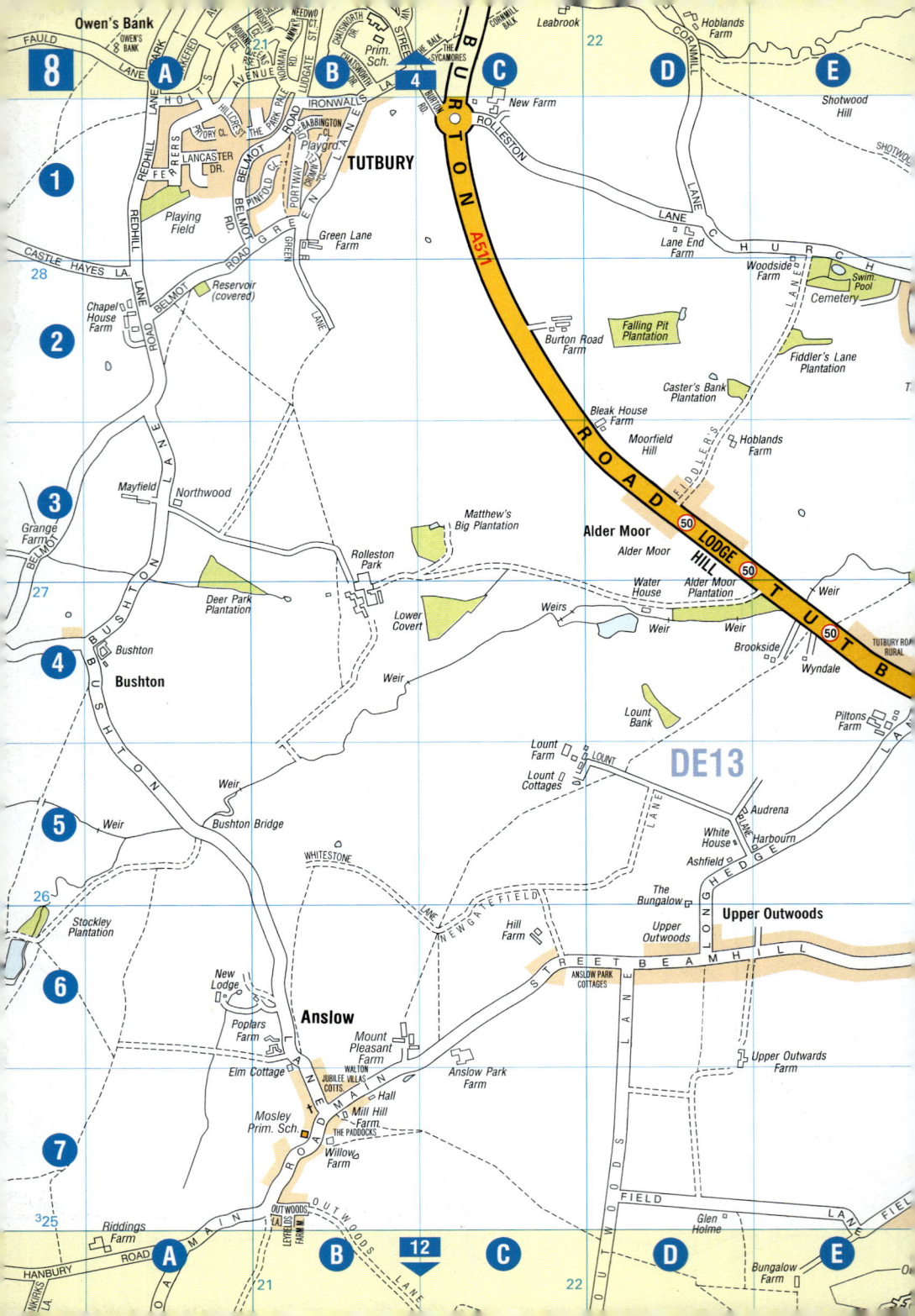

Owen's Bank
FAULD
OWEN'S BANK LANE

A   B   C   D   E

Leabrook   22   Hoblands Farm
CORNHILL BANK   CORNHILL
Shotwood Hill
SHOTWO...

1
New Farm
ROLLESTON
THE SYCAMORES
BURTON RD.
4
BURTON
TUTBURY
Prim. Sch.
IRONWALLS LA.
Playgrd.
BABBINGTON CL.
CROWN
GREEN
PORTWAY
PINFOLD CL.
BELMOT
THE PARK PALE
LANCASTER DR.
HILLCREST
PRIORY CL.
FERRERS
REDHILL LANE
HOLTS
AVENUE
CHATSWORTH DR.
LUDGATE ST.
CHATSWORTH
NEEDWOOD ST.
W. STREET
THE BALK
21
Playing Field

LANE   Lane End Farm
Woodside Farm
Cemetery
Swim. Pool

28
CASTLE HAYES LA.

2
Chapel House Farm
Reservoir (covered)
Green Lane Farm
BELMOT ROAD
BELMOT LANE
GREEN LANE
A511
Burton Road Farm
Falling Pit Plantation
Fiddler's Lane Plantation
Caster's Bank Plantation

3
Mayfield   Northwood
Grange Farm
BELMOT
BUSHTON LANE
Matthew's Big Plantation
Rolleston Park
Bleak House Farm
Moorfield Hill
Hoblands Farm
FIDDLER'S

27
Alder Moor
Alder Moor
ROAD
LODGE HILL
50

4
Bushton
Bushton
BUSHTON LANE
Deer Park Plantation
Lower Covert
Weir
Weirs
Water House
Alder Moor Plantation
Weir
Weir
Weir
Brookside
Wyndale
TUTBURY RD.
RURAL
50
TUTB...
Piltons Farm
LANE

5
Weir
Bushton Bridge
Weir
WHITESTONE
Lount Bank
Lount Farm
LOUNT
Lount Cottages
DE13
LANE
Audrena
White House
BLAKENHEDGE
Harbourn
Ashfield

26
Stockley Plantation
NEWGATEFIELD LANE
The Bungalow
Upper Outwoods
LONG HEDGE
Upper Outwoods

6
New Lodge
Poplars Farm
Anslow
Elm Cottage
LANE
Mount Pleasant Farm
WALTON
JUBILEE VILLAS
COTTS
Hill Farm
STREET
Anslow Park Cottages
BEAM HILL
Upper Outwards Farm

7
Mosley Prim. Sch.
ROAD MAIN
Hall
Mill Hill Farm
THE PADDOCKS
Willow Farm
Anslow Park Farm
LANE
STREET
FIELD
Glen Holme
WOODS
LANE FIE...

3 25
Riddings Farm
HANBURY
KINGS LA.
OUTWOODS LA.
LEYFIELDS FARM
OUTWOODS LANE
ROAD MAIN
Bungalow Farm

A   12   B   C   D   E
21   22

Map — Burton upon Trent / Rolleston on Dove area

F G H J K **9**

23 24 25 28

OLD RIVER DOVE

MARSTON LANE

RIVER DOVE

SOUTH DERBYSHIRE
EAST STAFFORDSHIRE

Mill Fleam

Home Farm
Home Farm Park

Sewage Works

Netherfield Grange

Cricket Ground
Pav.

1

2

MOSLEY MEWS
VIEW SHOTWOOD CL.
GLEBE
DOVELEA
ALDERS REACH
Ford
ALDERBROOK CL.
BROOKSIDE
STATION
CHAPEL LA.
SCHOOL
John of Rolleston Prim. Sch.
Prim. Sch. Play. Fld.
MEADOW VIEW
MEADOW
FOREST SCH.
WENTLANDS
WALFORD
SOUTH HILL
FAIRFIELD AV.
DOVECLIFF

Sunnymead Farm
Cliff House

THE LAWN
THE LAWNS
BURNS DR.
HAWKSLEY DR.
ELIZABETH AV.
BEACON AV.
KNOWLES
ROLLESTON ON DOVE
Sports Field

3
Dovecliff House

Weir
Brook Hollows Spinney
Stud Fm.
Brook Hollows
NEVILLE CL.
BEACON HILL
Beacon Hill
CRAYTHORNE ROAD

Sunnymead Farm

27 **10**

Club House
Cross Farm
Cross Lane
CRAYTHORNE GOLF COURSE
Craythorne Farm
Craythorne

STRETTON
CROXALL LANE
PRIOR
CHURCH
ALMOND
KNIGHTS
Hall
Cross
HILLFIELD

4

Burton upon Trent
Field Grove Farm
Oaklea
Elmleigh
Horninglow Cross
Small Holding
The Spinney Farm
ATHELSTAN
THE BEECHES
NENE CL.
SEVERN
GLEN AGE
SUNNINGDALE
ROLLESTON LANE
BARRINGTON CL.
LONGBOW
GOODWOOD
BELFRY
THE CHEVIN
HAM DR.
BRIDGE ST.
STATION
LADYWELL
HILLFIELD
WARREN CL.
BROOKE
HURST

5
26
Works

R 50
A511
Beam Hill
BEAM RD.
HAREHEDGE
Outwoods Prim. Sch.
The De Ferrers Academy (Dove Campus)
Play. Fld.
Playing Fields
Tennis Courts
The De Ferrers Academy (Trent Campus)
Play. Fld. De Ferrers
Prim. Sch.
BITHAM LANE
SHEEPWALK
BRITANNIA
ELWIN
FARADAY
A38
BEECH DRIVE
BEECH LA.
KINGSMEAD
Trent & Mersey Canal
Works
BRUNEL DRIVE
Works
EASTERN

6
Works

A511
ROAD
30
Play. Fld.
Green Valley Dr.
FOREST
EDGE WY.
RIDGE
GREAVES
BEACONSFIELD
FIELD RD.
Playing Field
Rec. Grd.
ST. MARY'S DR.
ST. LUKE'S RD.
ST. MARKS RD.
ST. JOHN'S
ST. FRANCIS
DE FERRERS
PRINCESS AV.
Works
DERBY
A5121 RD.
Club

7
DE14
Jun. Sch.
Burton Albion FC (Pirelli Stadium)
RYKNILD INDUSTRIAL ESTATE
Works

HORNINGLOW ROAD NTH.
Horninglow
ST. JOHN'S CL.
Beckett's Ct.
Curtis Ct.
HARPER
Rec. Ground
SHAKESPEARE
MAIN LINE IND. EST.
WETMORE

H F G H J K

Outwoods
QUEENS HOSPITAL
DADBY
RISE
HARBURY
FOSTON
BOSWORTH
DENTON
ASHFORD
WYGGESTON
CALAIS
DOVER
WESTFIELD
NORTON ST.
NORTHFIELD
13
MASEFIELD

23 24 25

26 A B 27 C D E

1

28

Ash Grove

Ceastree Farm
Egginton Lodge

BLACKSMITHS LA
DUCKLAKE
IVY CT.
OLD FGE CT.
ELM HURST
DOVE GRO.
6

STREET WILLIAM
NEWTON CL.
BRUNT'S
EGGINTON LANE

Manor Fm.
Peartree Farm
MAIN ST.
GRANGE
Whitehouse Farm
Grange Farm

FISHPOND LANE

Egginton

Eggington Hall

Playing Field

CHURCH ST.
Egginton Prim. Sch.

BROOK

Egginton Brook Bridge

Every Arms Farms

Eggir Cotta

RYKNILD STREET (Roman Road)

A38

2

Cliff House

Sewage Works

Benby House

CROSS MEWS

Rotherwood

ROAD

HILTON BROOK

DOVECLIFF

Weir
Dove Cliff

RIVER DOVE

Pumping Station
Lodge
High Bridge

3

nnymea Farm

Darfoulde House

Mill View

Clay Mills

Egginton Bridge

DERBY

Forge Poultry Farm

9 STRETTON

27

Monk's Bridge
Aqueduct

SOUTH DERBYSHIRE
EAST STAFFORDSHIRE

4

Primary Sch.

A38

DOVECLIFF ROAD
SIMS
HALL GREEN AV.
CROMWELL RD.
GAVIN WY.
DURHAM DR.
JORDAN AVENUE
SHREWSBURY RD.
BLADON
ROSE LA.
FORGE
CLAYMILLS
LAYMILLS VIEW

5

Hillfield

FIRHAM RD.
THORNE DR.
ALMOND
CLENTON
HALL
CROSS
WREN DRIVE
HILLFIELD LA.
AMBERLANDS
MOOR FURLONG
CHU. SCHWARD DR.
ALLERTON DR.
WHALLEY LA.
ALPINE WY.
MONCREIFF DR.

DE13

STREAM
MILL
Stream

6

Club

Trent & Mersey

Works

BRUNEL DRIVE
MILFORD DR.
PARK VW.
BRINDLEY WAY
Recreation Ground

A5121

MEADOW LA.

Filter Beds
Filter Beds

Claymills Pumping Station

Sewage Works

Burton upon Trent

RIVER TRENT

ROAD

7

Works

Ibion FC Stadium)

EASTERN AV.
BEECH AV.
HORTON AV.
JACKSON AV.
CORDEN AV.
THE HERDGREENS

DERBY ROAD

B5008

Lodge

NEWTON ROAD

Fish Ponds
Bothy Cottage

THE MEWS
NEWTON PARK

The Spinne

Cliffe Cottages
Cliffe Lodge

Castle Wood
Bladon Castle

Home Wood

25

RYKNILD INDUSTRIAL ESTATE

Works

MAIN LINE IND. EST.

Wetmoor Hall Farm

RIMBLING
HOPWOOD
CROSS ROAD
WETMORE

A Wetmore   B   **14**   C   D   E

26 Bladon Hill   27   Bladon Ho.   Newton Farm

Wrangland

The Bungalow
Nursery

F **G** **H** **J** **K**

CASTLE WAY
A5132 105
48 68

Willington

REPTON ROAD
7

29

TWYFORD ROAD
A5132
128 129

Prim. Sch.
TWYFORD AVENUE

WILLINGTON

Sandy Point

1

28

Green Plantation

Trent & Mersey Canal

Works

Willington Bridge

The Buries

Boat Ho.

2

WILLINGTON GRAVEL PITS NATURE RESERVE

Brook

Eggington

RIVER Trent

Derby DE65

WILLINGTON ROAD

B5008

Old Trent Water

Sports Ground
Swim. Pool
Sports Hall

School Ho.
Vic.

Repton School

Sports Ground

MONSOM LA.
MILTON RD.

3

27

INSET

St. Ann's Well

TANNER'S LA.

ROAD

Playing Fields

Repton School
The Cross
The Abbey
LATHAM HO.
THE GARDEN
Sch.
NEW HO.

BROOK END

THE PRIORY
BROOK HO.

MERCIA CT.
RICHMOND ST.

4

Parson's Hills

Playing Field
FIELD HO.

B5008 ROAD

CHESTNUT

THE MITRE

The Knoll

BURTON

Hill Top Farm

Cokhay

Cokhay Green

43

MITRE DR.
THE

REPTON

SPINNEY

WAY

WELL

Tennis Court

BROOMHILLS LA.

Playing Field
Pav.

5

Recreation Ground

Trent Farm

Blacksmiths
CRICKET
MILL
HOLMES

B5008 ROAD

REPTON ST.
NEWTON END

Newton Solney

Grange Farm

DE15

The Hill Farm

LANE

F **G** 15 **H**
29

INSET

B5008 WILLINGTON ROAD

Old Trent Water

Brook Farm

Monsom Farm

Cemy

6

Swim. Pool

School Ho.
Vic.

Repton School

Sports Ground

MONSOM LA.

Derby DE65

Sports Hall

Playing Fields

The Cross
Repton School
The Abbey

B5008 RD.

BURTON

NEW HO.

THE MITRE

Sch.

THE PRIORY

BROOK END
MILTON RD

The Dales

Askew House

Prim.

327

7

MERCIA CT.
RICHMOND ST.

PINFOLD LA. MT. PLEASANT RD

REPTON

WAY

WELL

J **K**

Tennis Court

Playing Field

430

31

1 **2** **3** **4** **5** **6** **7**

12

A **B** **8** **C** **D** **E**

21

22

Anslow

Lower Outwoods

Burton upon Trent

Riddings Farm

Willow Farm

Glen Holme

Bungalow Farm

NANNIKS LA.

HANBURY

Common Farm

CHAPEL LA.

Henhurst Field

Redhouse Farm

Reservoirs (covered)

1

2

Leyfields Farm

Henhurst Wood Farm

Shobnall Brook

Henhurst Wood

Bungalow Farm

Keepers Cottage

HENHURST FARM

Oakhurst

Oaks Wood

PEGG COURT 249

30

238

Hall

HENHURST

B5017

HILL FOREST

DINGLE

HIGHCROFT

Shobnall Prim. Sch.

ROAD SHOBN

A38

3

Rough Hay

Playing Field

89

88

AVIATION

Shobnall Dingle

Shobnall

OAKS GRANGE

BROOM WAY

Reservoir

RESERVOIR ROAD

HENHURST RIDGE

Council Depot

Shobnall Grange

Bowling Grn.

Pav.

Sub.

Bow Gree

4

24

Postern House Farm

Sandyford Dingle

Sinai Park

Tennis Cts.

Sports Grd.

Glenfield

DE13

SINAI PARK

Lord's Well

CALLISTER

Warehouse

FOURTH AV.

Trent

5

23

CALLINGWOOD LA.

Pool Green Farm

The Rough

Depot

The Thorns

Warehouse

Prince's Covert

WATERSIDE CT.

SKYLINE

6

COMMON

School Bridge

NEW ROW

The Bungalows

Works

SEVENTH AV.

CENTRUM ONE HUNDRED

MERCIA PARK

7

22

PARK

Hall

Battlestead Hill

Park Pale

TATENHILL

Manor Farm

The Mill House

Lawns Farm

Lawns Farm Cottage

Branston Lock

Superstore

CENTRUM EAST RETAIL PARK

Health Club

CROWN SQ.

CLAY'S

CLEWLEY

HARWOOD

HARWOOD

WELLINGTON

Rec. Grd.

BRANSTO

Yews Bridge

BRANSTON

BRANSTON ROAD

Branston Bridge

A38

A5121

FARADAY

FESTIVAL

Grave Yard

A **B** **18** **C** **D** **E**

21

22

BURTON UPON TRENT

Outwoods

QUEENS HOSPITAL

Midlands Treatment Centre

Outwoods Hills

Shobnall

Shobnall Sports Complex

Paddling Pool

Burton on-Trent

Wetmore

Little Burton

The National Brewery Centre

Burton & Derbyshire College

Bond End

Stapenhill

Uxbridge Pleasure Ground

Birmingham Curve Junction

Meadowside Leisure Centre

Trent Washlands

St. Modwen's Orchard

Ox Hay Pleasure Ground

Horse Holme

Upper Mills Farm

DE14

DE15

A5121 A5189 A5018 A511 A38 B5017 B5018 B6017 B5416 B5189

14

A B C D E

10

Cliffe Cottages
Castle Well
Cottage
The Spinn...

Works
Wetmoor Hall Farm
Wetmore

Castle Well
Bladon Castle
Bladon Hill
Bladon Ho. School
The Lodge
The Close
THE HOUSES
THE RIDGE
BLADON

Wranglands Plantation
Newtor...

1

NILD INDUSTRIAL ESTATE
Works
MAIN LINE IND. EST.
RIVERSIDE PARK
HOPWOOD
Works
Rec. Grd.

ROAD
B5008

Bladon Paddocks
Bladon Farm
Victory Plantation

2

ELECTRIC ST. IND. EST.
APS IND. PK. Depot WORK EST.
GRANARY WHARF BUS. PK.
Depot
Weir
Cricket Ground
Meadows Farm
Pipe Line
Mill Stream
Dale
Bladon Farm Cottages

Ford

DE14

3

HCM IND. EST.
Fitness First
Sports Grd.
Bowl. Grn.
Tennis Courts
Tennis Cts.
Recreation Ground
Tennis Courts

WINSHILL

Abbot Beyne Sch. (Evershed Building)
Playing Fields
Abbot Beyne Sch. (Linnell Building)
Play. Flds.
Redmoor

HAWFIELD
Prim. Sch.

HAWFIELD

13

4

BRIDGE ST.
A511
TRENT BRI.
Weir
Burton Bridge
Meadowside Leisure Centre
River Centre

BEARWOOD
NEWTON
HILL
CHURCH ROAD
High
ST. CANTERBURY

Tower View Prim. Sch.
Madras Rd.
Play. Fld.
The Limes

5

Trent Washlands
Modwer Orchard
The Greenhouse Gardening & Environmental Cen.
Cemetery
Scalpcliff Hill
Waterloo Clump
Waterloo Mount
Tower Woods

A511
ROAD AS...
MOAT BANK

Pleasure Ground
Playing Field
Pav.

6

Horse Holme
THE CLOISTERS
ST. PETER'S
STAPENHILL
War Mem.
MALVERN ST.
MALVERN AVENUE
GRAFTON
BEAUFORT

Brizlincote Hall Farm

EAST STAFFORDSHIRE
SOUTH DERBYSHIRE

7

BRIDGE
JERRAM'S
ST. PETER'S STREET
STANTON
A444
HOLLY
The Wickets

STAPENHILL

Forest Dell
Model Dairy Farm
Pit (dis)
Cave
Pit (dis)

The Violet Way Academy

A B C D E

20

Paulet High School
Playing

11

325

Dale Farm

Cockey Barn

Derby DE65

Broken Flats

1

Beaconhill Plantation

Falders Cottages

Hill Farm

2

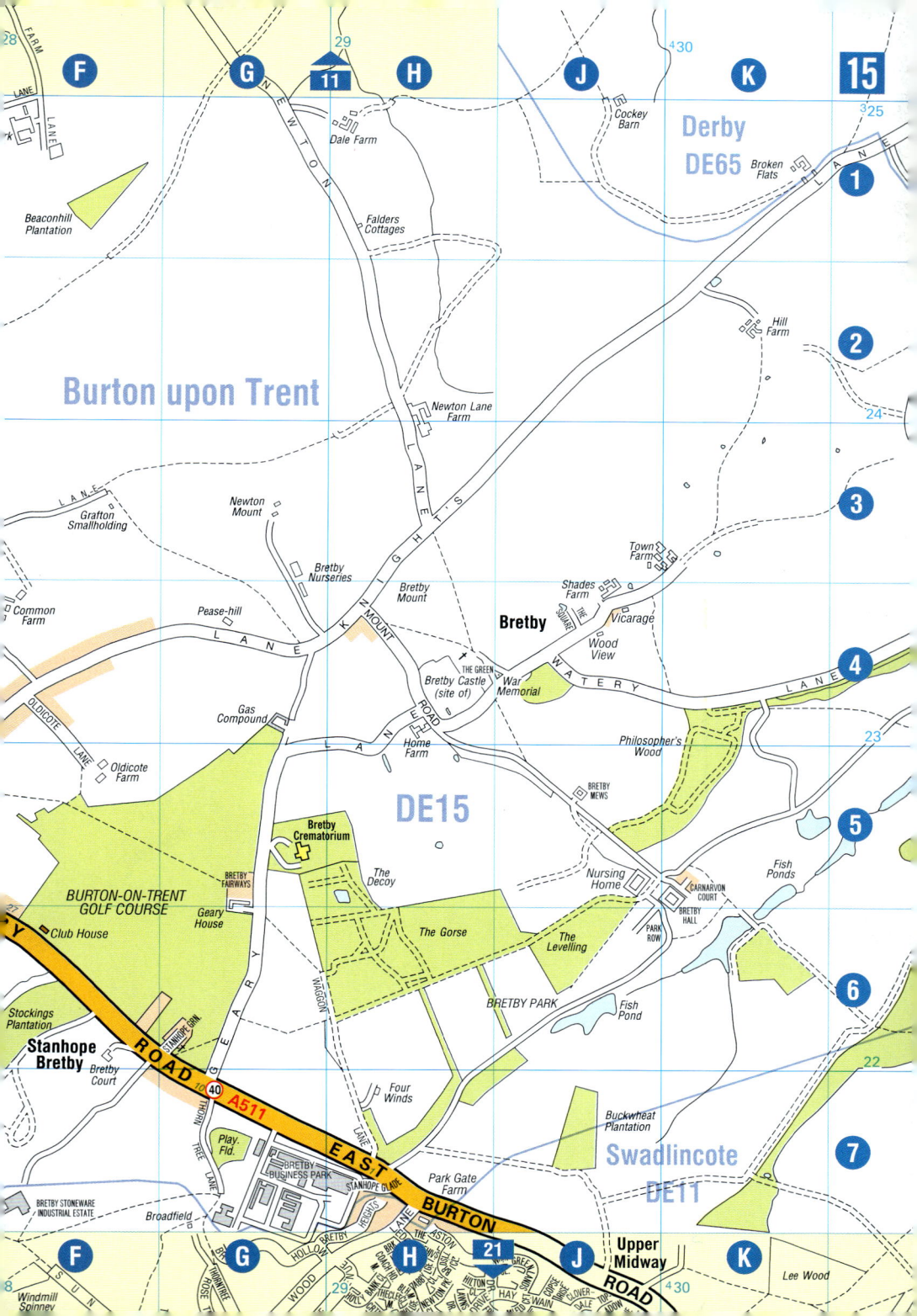

Burton upon Trent

Newton Lane Farm

24

Grafton Smallholding

Newton Mount

LANE

KEIGHTS

3

Town Farm

Bretby Nurseries

Pease-hill

Bretby Mount

Shades Farm

THE SQUARE

Vicarage

Common Farm

LANE

K MOUNT

Bretby

Wood View

LANE

4

THE GREEN

W A T E R Y

Bretby Castle (site of)

War Memorial

23

OLDICOTE LANE

Gas Compound

ROAD

Home Farm

Philosopher's Wood

Oldicote Farm

LANE

Bretby Mews

Fish Ponds

DE15

Bretby Crematorium

5

Bretby FAIRWAYS

The Decoy

Nursing Home

CARNARVON COURT

BURTON-ON-TRENT GOLF COURSE

Geary House

The Gorse

PARK ROW

Bretby HALL

GEARY

The Levelling

6

Stockings Plantation

Stanhope Bretby

Club House

STANHOPE GRM

WAGGON

Fish Pond

BRETBY PARK

22

Bretby Court

A511

TO

40

ROAD

Four Winds

Buckwheat Plantation

7

Play. Fld.

THORN FREE LANE

E A S T

Bretby Business Park

STANHOPE GLADE

Park Gate Farm

Swadlincote DE11

Bretby STONEWARE INDUSTRIAL ESTATE

Broadfield

B U R T O N

Windmill Spinney

Upper Midway

ROAD

Lee Wood

8

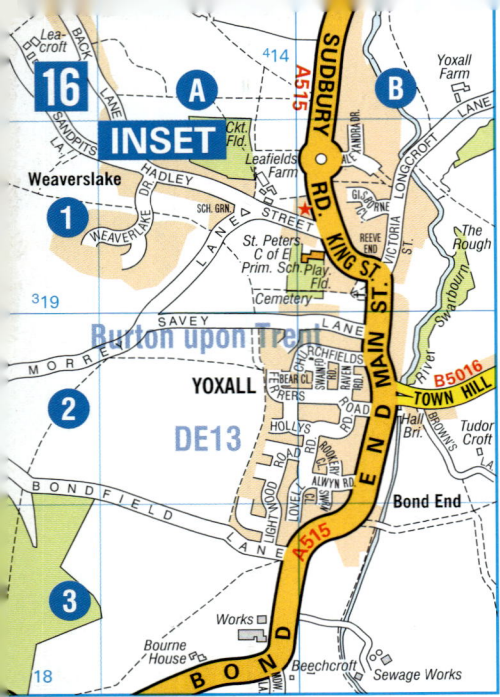
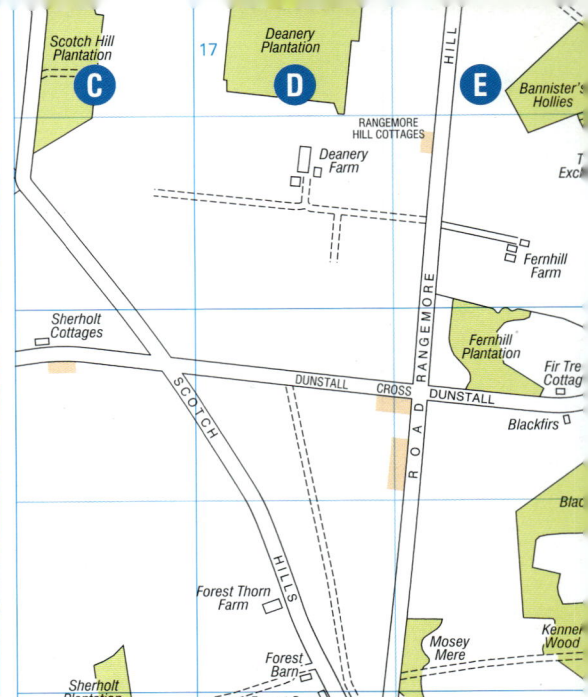

F   G   H   J   **TATENHILL**   K

The Oaks
Fox Holes
Robinson's Plantation
MOORES

ROBIN HOOD COTTS
MAIN ST
MANOR CFT
BRANSTON RD
THE WOODS
SOWNY LA
THE GROVE

1

Sprinks Barn Farm
Bikersdale Wood

21

The Larches
The Hills
Greenlane Plantation
DUNSTALL

2

The Priory
The Orchard
Church Villas
Home Farm House
The Lady Pond
The Park

Old Hall
The Oaks
The Elms
Dunstall Hall
Pav.
The Rookery
Black Meadow Wood

320

3

18

The Kennels
Mill Pond
Dunstall
Ckt. Grd.
Lower Farm

4

Saw Mill Cott.
The Old School House
The Pool
ROAD
ARMITAGE
HILL

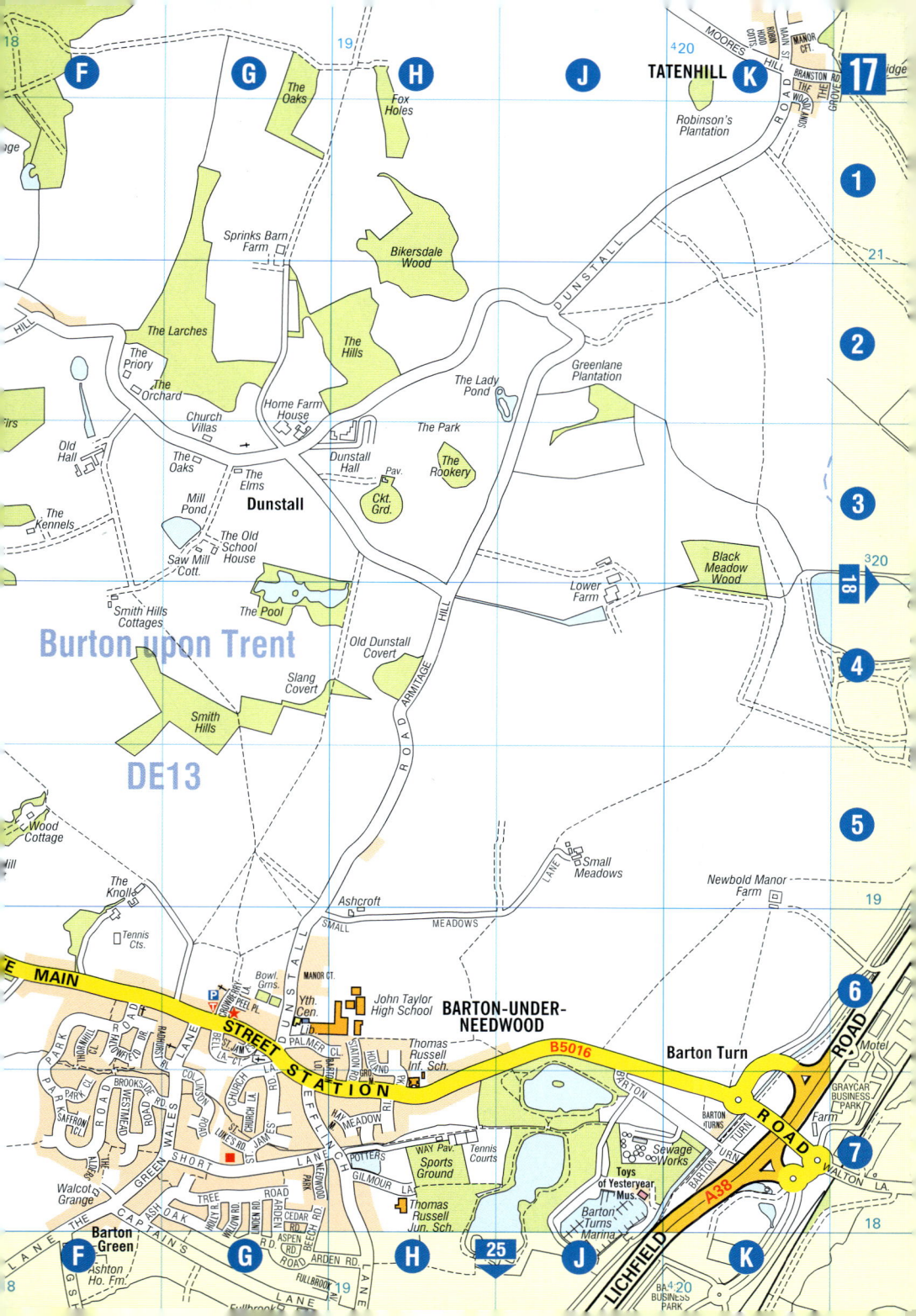

Burton upon Trent

Smith Hills Cottages
Old Dunstall Covert

19

DE13

Slang Covert
Smith Hills

5

Wood Cottage
Small Meadows
Newbold Manor Farm

The Knoll
Tennis Cts.
Ashcroft
SMALL
MEADOWS
LANE

19

THE MAIN
P
Bowl. Grns.
MANOR CT.
John Taylor High School
BARTON-UNDER-NEEDWOOD
ROAD
Motel
GRAYCAR BUSINESS PARK

6

STREET STATION
DUNSTALL
Yth. Cen.
Lib
Thomas Russell Inf. Sch.
Barton Turn
Farm

CANON'RY LA
PEEL PL.
BELL
ST. JAMS
PALMER CL
B5016
BARTON
BARTON TURNS
ROAD

7

Walcot Grange
ST. JAMES
HOLLOWAY
HAY MEADOW
POTTERS
Sports Ground
Tennis Courts
Sewage Works
Toys of Yesteryear Mus.
BARTON TURN
WALTON LA.

Barton Green
Ashton Ho. Fm.
F
G
Thomas Russell Jun. Sch.
H
Barton Turns Marina
J
LICHFIELD   ROAD
A38
K

WAY Pav.
GILMOUR LA.
TREE
HOLLY RD
WILLOW RD
LINDEN RD
CEDAR RD
ARDEN RD
ASPEN RD
BEECH RD
FULLBROOK RD

25

18

PARK
NORMANHILL
BROOKSIDE
WESTMEAD
SAFFRON TCL
BRETBY HILL
GREEN WALES
SHORT
CAPTAIN'S
THE
KINGS
8
19

F G H **13** J Upper Mills Farm K **19**

Depot Depot
Depot Depot Cricket Grd.
Depot Depot Rec. Grd. Pav. Bowling Grn. SAXON

BRANSTON LEICESTER BLACKPOOL
ROAD **30** Play. Fld. Comm. Cen. HEATH
B5018 Prim. Sch. STAPENHILL **1**

Cricket Ground Pav. **2**
Paget High School, Business and Enterprise College Driving Range The Rookery

BRANSTON GOLF COURSE Boat House

Club House R I V E R   T R E N T The Verge Playing Field Football Ground **3**

Old Hall Cottages Factory **20** **320**

The Wilderness Drakelowe House

Water Treatment Plant Home Farm **Drakelow** **4**

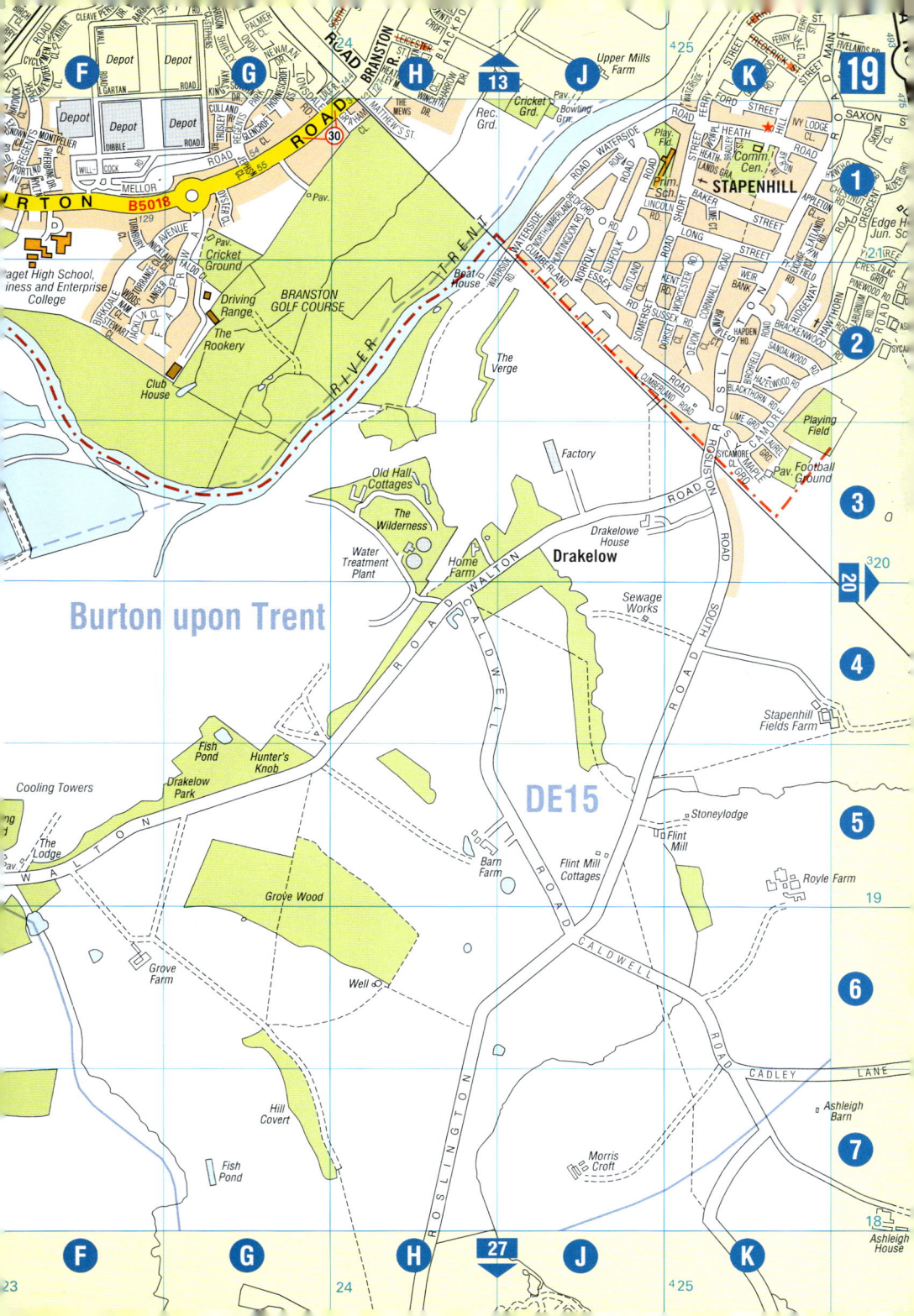

Burton upon Trent Sewage Works Stapenhill Fields Farm

Fish Pond Hunter's Knob **DE15** Stoneylodge **5**

Cooling Towers Drakelow Park Flint Mill Royle Farm 19

The Lodge Barn Farm Flint Mill Cottages **6**

Grove Wood Well

Grove Farm CADLEY LANE Ashleigh Barn

Hill Covert Morris Croft **7**

Fish Pond **18** Ashleigh House

F G H **27** J K

23 24 25

STAPENHILL

A B C D E

1

The Violet Way Academy
Paulet High School
SAXON ST
STANTON
A444
Ivy Lodge Cl
FERRY
MAIN
REET
HILL Road
COMLEY CL
IVELANDS RD.
VIOLET
ENVALE CL
ORCHARD
MINSTON ST
DERBY RD
HAZELDENE
S. WAY
HILSDALE
PAULET
SCH. DR.
JASMINE
HOME CR.
HW

21
Edge Hill Jun. Sch.
CHESTNUT
POLLSTON
APPLETON
WITHORN
RIDGEWAY
CRESCENT
ALDER GRO
CRES
LILAC
PINEWOOD
LABURNUM
ASPEN M.
CHESTNUT CL
YEW TREE
TREE
BLUE STONE LA
30
A444
ROAD
BRETLANDS
MEAD WK
MEAD
DR
MANOR
CR
MANOR
Blessed Robert Sutton Catholic Sports College

14

27

The Shrubbery

2
Heath Farm
SYCAMORE CT.
SANDALWOOD
HAWTHORN
HAZELWOOD
SYC
BIRCH
EAST STAFFORDSHIRE
SOUTH DERBYSHIRE
ROAD
WOODLAND
Depot
PIDDOCKS
ROAD
Stanton Manor
Manor Farm
Newhall Wood

3
Playing Field
Pav.
Football Ground
320
19
Burton upon Trent
DE15
Hill Farm
30
A444
STANTON
Playing Fld.
Stanton Primary School
Rifle Range
WOODVIEW RD
WATE LA.
SOPWELLS RD
B5353

4
Stanton House Cotts
Stanton House
BRIDLE
LANE
Depot
Playing Field
29
PARK
A444
30
Hallfields Farm
HALLFIELDS RD.
Hall Fields Farm
TETRON POINT GOLF COURSE

5
Stapenhill Fields Farm
Weir
Junction Spinney
Royle Farm
19
Sewage Works
Council Farm
Works
Tetron Point

6
Spring (Chalybeate)
Breach Farm
Cadley Hill Farm
Cadley Hill
ROAD
BURTON
CADLEY HILL
CADLEY
A514
UPPER GLADE
RYDER
CADLEY HILL INDUSTRIAL ESTATE
PB'S

7
Ashleigh Barn
Breach Cottage
CADLEY
LANE
CADLE
LANE
DE12
Grasmere
COTON
A444
SNADT

18
Ashleigh House
A
SANDY
Hill Crest Farm
B
New Barn Farm
28
C
Works
D
PARK
CASTLE GRESLEY
HOME FARM
MOUNT
E
26
27

Swadlincote

MIDWAY

NEWHALL

CHURCH GRESLEY

SWADLINCOTE

DE 11

Upper Midway

Lee Wood

Windmill Spinney

Broadfield

William Allitt School

Play. Flds. Newhall Inf. Sch.

Newhall Jun. School

Parliament

Cemetery

Playing Field

Midway Farm

Springfield

Elmsleigh Inf. Sch.

Junior Sch.

Eureka

Eureka Park

Training Centre

Playing Field

The Pingle School

Fairmeadows Prim. School

Hawfields Farm

Breach Leys Farm

DARKLANDS

Works

Depot

HIGH STREET

ST. UNION RD. NEWHALL

B5353 ROAD

B5586

A51

A514 NADIN WILLIAM WAY CIVIC WAY

DERBY RD.

MIDWAY ST. CHURCH ST.

MAIN ROAD

Club House

Gresley Office Pk.

Depot

Works

George Holmes Business Park

Astron Business Park

EVISA

Heathcote Road Ind. Est.

Council Offices

Leisure Cen.

Superstore

Mus.

Odeon

Superstore

Rink

Swadlincote Ski & Snowboard Centre

Ski Slope

Woodland

Playing Fields

Jack i' th' Holes

Gresley Common

Works

Depot

Boardman Ind. Est.

Oaktree Business Park

The Woodlands Kids Rough

Appleby Glade Industrial Estate

Pennine Way Junior Academy

Cemetery

Playing Field

Club

Memorial Park

Bandstand

Mem.

Comm. Cen.

Gresley Old Hall

Sports Ground

Church Gresley Indoor Bowls Centre

Sports Ground

Hall Wood

Sports Ground

Gresley FC (The Moat Grd.)

Albert Village

War Mem.

Albert Village Prim. Sch.

Pool Works

Colliery Row

Depot

Church Gresley Ind. Est.

Recreation Ground

Station

A **B** 31 **C** 32 **D** **E**

1
Lee Wood
MIDWAY
21
Nether Hall
Brick House Farm
Hall Farm
SPRINGHILL COTTAGES
Springhill
Hartshorne
A514
TICKNALL ROAD

Dunnsmoor Farm
DUNNSMOOR
NETHERHALL ROAD
REPTON LANE
BROOK STREET
PEAR TREE CL
MILLPOND
ADAMS CL
KENDRICKS CL
MANOR VW
Manor Farm

2
Lower Midway
BURTON ROAD
SANDCLIFFE
COVENTRY
WINCHESTER DR
Eureka Prim. Sch.
SALISBURY
DURHAM
DRIVE
TRURO CL
South Lodge
LINCOLN
Hartshorne C of E Prim. Sch.
Recreation Ground
MAIN ST
ROAD
MANCHE
SLACK
St. PETERS
CHURCH

3
MIDWAY
Playing Field
A511
SKINNERS
WAY
GRANVILLE
MASON CT
THOMPSON CL
Granville Sports College
Playing Field
Broomy Furlong
Goseley Dale
TOWER RD
A514
WOODVILLE RD

Swadlincote DE11
Fox Covert

4
CHURCH
DERBY
VICARAGE
BODICOTE WAY
HOLE WAY
MANSFIELD CL
SORREL
WOOD FM LA
The Sycamores
Olders Valley
Playing Field
Nursery
Swadlincote Woodlands Forest Park
HARTSHORNE RD
WOODVILLE RD A514
Goseley Estate
Comm Cen
NINELANDS
BROOKDALE RD
ELMSDALE RD
Playing Field
Nielands Mobile Home Park
EDWARD ST
Hilltop Farm

5
Ski Slope
Swadlin Ski & Snowboard Centre
Playing Field
19
SWADLINCOTE
A514
SWADLINCOTE ROAD
CROWN
138
Works
OLD TOLL
HIGH ST
Suttons Business Park
Wks
VIKING BUS CEN
Woodville
SOUTH DERBYSHIRE
NORTH WEST LEICESTERSHIRE
Reservoir (covered)

6
COMMON
Jack i' th' Holes
POOL
Gresley Comm
Granville Industrial Estate
Works
Vicarage
Rec. Grd.
Schools
NEW RD
MOIRA LANE
STAPTON PK IND EST
Little Thorns Industrial Estate
A511 STREET ASHBY
FOREST RD
Blackfordby House
Blackfor St. Margaret Prim. S

7
A30 Albert Village
OCCUPATION
Works
Pool Works
Works
A30
Albert Village Prim. Sch.
MOIRA LANE
The Rookery
MEAKIN DR
DAVENPORT
NORTH
ROAD
ELSTEAD RD
FENTON
The Furlongs

A 31 **B** 30 **C** 32 **D** **E**
LITTLEWORTH
BOOTHORPE

F | G | H | J | K

Coppice Farm

White Hollows Farm
Archer's Alders
435

Shaw's Alders

Derby
DE73

Tadsor Farm

Pisternhill Plantation

Ladyfields Plantation

Heath Farm

Limehouse Dam

The Elms
Long Alders

1

21

2

B5006

Daniel Hay Farm

Pistern Hills

Pisternhill Plantation

HORN HILL

Sharp's Bottom

Pistern Hill

Pisternhill Farm

LANE

3

END

320

Several Wood

LANE

Stables
Reservoir (covered)

HEATH

4

Short Hazels Farm

Several Woods Farm

Heath Farm

Hartshorne Heath

Pistern Hills Farm East

Reservoir (covered)

LANE

FORTIES

Park Place

Ashby-de-la-Zouch

The Forties

Play-Field

Stonehouse Farm

Mount House

Smisby

5

Hedgefield Farm

Water Tower

Tithe Farm

217

Manor Farm

CHAPEL ST.
MAIN

Rose Mount

19

40

R O A D

152

A511
Boundary

ASHBY - DE - LA - ZOUCH

Myrtle Lodge Farm

LE65

ROAD

OLD
PARKS

LANE

6

B5006

SMISBY RD.

Woodcote

Scam-Hazel Farm

Sewage Works

A511

BY-PASS

SMISBY

Gilwiskaw Brook

The Bungalow

7

Scam-Hazel Wood

Rose Cottage

Annwell House

ANNWELL

ANNWELL PLACE

Holywell Farm

IVANHOE BUSINESS PARK

IVANHOE PARK WY.

Works

CLIFTONTHORPE MDWS.

STREET HEATH

Blackfordby Hall

Lady Wood

BURTON ROAD

TOM BILL

Works

Depot
Dairy

BLACKFORDBY

F | G | H | J | K

Newlands

Prestop Park Farm

31
INGLES CROSSING SITE

34

Ingles Hill Farm

435

IVANHOE INDUSTRIAL ESTATE

Works

Depot

Depot

WAY

ROAD

IVAN INDUSTR

8

A B C D E
1 2 3 4 5 6 7

High-hall-hill Plantation
Keepers Cottage
The Coppice
16
Parkhill Plantation
Blakenhall Park
Blakenhall Cottage
Park Bungalow
Gorsey Hill Farm

The Faggness
Colonel's Plantation

The Ashes
Baggaley's Wood
Woodyard Spinney
Pool Tail Spinney

Burton upon Trent
DE13

River Swarbourn
Coach House
Wychnor Manor
WYCHNOR PARK

RIVER TRENT

Lady's Walk
Lawn Bank House
Lawn Bank

Hill Cottages
GREEN

Wychnor Hill Farm
Wychnor
Equestrian Centre
Cunnary Farm

EAST STAFFORDSHIRE
LICHFIELD

Weir RIVER TRENT

Works
OVERLEY LANE
WHITE HEART MEWS
Overley
Pyford Brook Cottage

Trent & Mersey Canal
Essington House Farm
ALREWAS

A513

Pyford Brook
315

Gaskell's Bridge
Crackpotz
MICKLEHOME DRIVE
Works
The Homestead

Mill Acres House

Kent's Bridge
Bagnall Lock
Cricket Ground
Pav
All Saints' C of E Prim. Sch.

KINGS BROMLEY

Bagnall

R Y K N E L D — A38
(ROMAN RD)

Underpass

D A I S Y L A N E
FOX LANE
LONG LA
16 17
A513

F · G · H · J · K

18
19

Walton
Potters

WAY Pav.
Sports
Ground

Tennis
Courts

Sewage
Works

Toys
of Yesteryear
Mus.

Barton
Turns
Marina

GILMOUR

Thomas
Russell
Jun. Sch.

17

420

ROAD

LICHFIELD

A38

Barton
Green

Ashton
Ho. Fm.

CASTLE
SHORT
GREEN
TREE
OAK
NEEDWOOD
MILL
CEDAR
ASPEN
ARDEN
FULLBROOK
ARDEN RD.

BARTON-UNDER-
NEEDWOOD

BARTON
BUSINESS
PARK

Depot

18

1

Bridleway
Cottage

Fullbrook
Farm

Fullbrook

MILL
SAWDRAY
MILL DR.
HARDY CL.
LANE

Borough
Holme

2

DOGSHEAD
LANE
CAPTAIN'S
LANE

Bonthorne
Farm

Efflinch

Catholme
Bridge

Trent & Mersey Canal

Depot

17

3

EFFLINCH
LANE
CATHOLME
LANE

Catholme

Catholme

26

4

Wychnor
Bridges

A38

Wychnor
Lock

Wychnor
Bridges
Farm

16

Pebble
Mill

5

STREET
LANE

Willowbrook Farm
(CAMPING & CARAVAN SITE)

Catton
Hall

Ga
C

Cherry
Holme

Swadlincote
DE12

6

Sewage
Works

315

RIVER
TRENT

SOUTH
DERBYSHIRE
LICHFIELD

Catton Wood

7

National
Memorial Arboretum

Visitor
Centre

UN
Spiral

Armed Forces
Memorial

Mytholme
Cottage

Lichfield
WS13

Croxall
Wood

F · G · H · J · K

18
19
420

A B C D E

DE13

EAST STAFFORDSHIRE
SOUTH DERBYSHIRE

RIVER STATION LA.
Bridge
WALTON
Rectory
MAIN
MEWIES CL.
Barn Farm
Hill Croft
Walton Hall
Walton-on-Trent
C of E Prim. Sch.

WALTON-ON-TRENT

Fairfield

1

18

DE13

Borough Holme

Borough Hill

The Dumps

Windmill Bank

Marlpit Spinney

Walton Hill Farm

Ashtree Farm

2

17

Coppershill Spinney

Ryelands Lodge

Playing Field

Pav.

Walton Wood

Swadlincote

DE12

Oaklands Farm

Twin Oaks House

3

25

RIVER TRENT

Ryelands Plantation

Round Lodge

Black Plantation

Borough Fields Farm

Borough Fields Cottage

4

16

5

The Rough

Donkhill Cottages

Catton Farm Cottages

Cherry Holme

Gardeners Cottage

Catton Hall

Catton

Donkhill Plantation

Clarence Cottage

Summerfields

6

315

Catton Park

The Woodlands

Donkhill Farm

Mansditch Cottage

King's Covert

7

Catton Wood

Longs Cottage

Mansditch Farm

A B C D E

SOUTH DERBYSHIRE
LICHFIELD

Brook Plantation

21 22

23 24 4 25

Fish Pond

Morris Croft

shleig. House

18

Burton upon Trent DE15

ROSLISTON ROAD

1

Corner Farm

Caldwell

MAIN ST.

Priory Farm

LA. ND

anor Fa

Walton Lane Farm

Calves Croft Farm

CHURCH LA.

2

Pegasus School

17

Moonraker

BURTON RD.

Caldwell Covert

THE CHASE

THE GLEN

VICARAGE

MAIN

Sch.

Playing Field

3

ROAD

THE HOLLOW

WELLAN

YEW TREE RD.

YEW TREE

GS.

CHAPEL CFT.

Cinderlands

Crossfields Lodge

28

C

ROSLISTON

Play Fld.

CHAPEL ST.

NEW ST.

Willow Farm

STRAWBERRY

Sports Field Pav.

4

STREET LANE

LINTON RD.

LINTON

Works

Works

16

Field House Farm

COTON

Malt House Farm

Longfurlong Farm

Beehive Farm Woodland Lake

Caravan Site.

ROAD

CATTON

Lads Grave

Brook

5

Pessall

Overfields Farm

Church Farm

CHURCH CROFT

OAK TREE CL.

RD.

ELMS

Prim. Sch.

CHAPEL ST.

COAL

6

Greenacre Park

Play Fld.

Playgrd.

CHURCH

ELMS

GLEBE VIEW

CHAMMANS

BURTON ST.

Works

BARNS CT.

ST.

MILL GRN

MILL ROAD

COTON IN THE ELMS

PIT

LANE

CRAFTY FLATS LA.

3 15

7

Garland's Wood

Malt House Farm

LITTLE LIVERPOOL

Church Flatts Farm

Cara Pa

23 24 4 25

18

A **B** **20** **C** **D** **E**

Grasmere

Ashleigh House

Hill Crest Farm

New Barn Farm

Works

CASTLE GRESLEY

HOME FARM RD

SCOTTS

THE

MOUNT

1

COTON PARK

Coton Park

Sewage Works

Coton

Priory Farm

MAIN STREET

CHURCH LANE

SANDY LANE

2

Manor Farm

Caldwell

Recreation Ground

Swadlincote

17

Pegasus School

dwell vert

GRANGE FARM COURT

Manor Farm

Manor House

PARK HILLSIDE

PARK CL

3

C A L D W E L L

R O A D

PEAR TREE DR

MAIN STREET

ROAD 27

Privet Plantation

WARREN DR

LIGHTFIELDS

CHESTRD GREENWD

CEDAR

PRINCESS

THE CLOSE

CRES

CARLTON

SYCAMORE

WINDSOR

HESSON

WINCHESTER

PATRICK

EMERY

FRED

WEATHERN

GRANGEWD DR

STREET

LINTON

Vic.

Rec. Grd.

Play Fie

4

Blakenhall Farm

Longlands

Sports Field

16

HIGH

Netherleigh

5

P

Far Close Farm

Oak Dene

COLLIERY LANE

Woodside Farm

Hill Far

DE12

6

Botany Bay Farm

Botany Bay

FLATS LANE

Park Farm

315

CRAFTY

LANE

Potter's Wood

7

The Ashes

GRANGE WOOD

Caravan Park

sh Flatts arm

A **B** **C** **D** **E**

26

27

Grangewood Farm

F G H 21 J K

Albert Village Prim. Sch.

Albert Village **1**

High Cross Bank

HIGH

BURTON RD

CASTLE

Princess Street

Station Street

Bank St

Chattens Mow

Recreation Ground

DE11

Church Gresley Wood

Depot Church Gresley Industrial Estate

Factories

Play. Fld.

18 THE CLOSE

17 **2**

Air Shaft

Tunnel Woods

Gresley Tunnel

Air Shaft

MOUNT PLEASANT

Arnold Cl.

Mount Pleasant

CROSS

Linnet Learning Cen.

Swainspark Wood

Swainspark

SWAINSPARK INDUSTRIAL ESTATE

OCCUPATION ROAD

Clay Pit **3**

30 ROAD **3**

Greenfields

Shortwoods

Waterfallows Farm

Park Road Mobile Home Park

THE CONIFERS

PARK ROAD

NORTH WEST LEICESTERSHIRE

SOUTH DERBYSHIRE

Depot

Works

COTTAGE ROAD

4

16

Linton Heath

HEATH ROAD

De Ferrers Pl.

Pav. Sports Grd.

BURTON

ROAD

Primary School

LINTON

Sealwood

Scal View

GREEN LANE

Middle Hayes Farm

A444

Orchard View

SLACKEY LANE

SPRING ROAD

HARTSHORNE ROAD

STANLEY ROAD

Alexandra Ct.

Alexandra Rd

Edward St

Royal

The Elms

5

LANE

Hooborough

Sealwood Cottage

LANE

GREEN

ROAD

Sealwood Farm

Woodside Cottage

OVERSEAL

Coronation St

Woodlands Av

Oaklands St

West Vw

WOODVILLE ROAD

HALLCROFT

Hall Playing Fields

Church Farm

DAISY

Overseal Prim. Sch. Playing Field

Gorsey Leys

Gorsey Leys Farm

Gorsey Leys

MANOR STABLES

MANOR AV

Poplars Farm

BATH ROAD

SHORT LANE

Blencathra

Brook

LANE

Lagoona Park

Brooklands Farm

6

30

LULLINGTON ROAD

VALLEY ROAD

BRAMMEL WLK

CLIFTON WLK

BAILEY

ASHLEY CL

SQUIRREL WLK

JACKSON CL

Acresford View

SCHOOL LANE

MOIRA ROAD

MAIN ST

A444

ACRESFORD RD

The Shrubbery

Shortheath Farm

Short Heath

Woodview Farm

Short 15

7

Gunby Lea

GUNBY HILL

Grangewood Nursery and Craft Centre

CHURCH

Hooborough

Sewage Works

F G H J K

29 30

A   **B**   **22**   **C**   **D**   **E**

31   32

Wall Mem

Albert Village Prim. Sch.

18

30

THE CLOSE

LITTLEWORTH

1

OCCUPATION

MUSHROOM LANE

MOIRA

DE11

Boothorpe Farm

Boothorpe Hall

BOOTHORPE

Works

The Furlongs

FENTON

STRAWBERRY LANE

NORTH CL

SOUTH CL

HALSTEAD

CHURCH

LANE WELL

MAIN

THORNTON

SANDTOP

BRIAR

BLACKFORDBY

2

RESERVOIR

Feanedock Covert

17

Norrishill Farm

DRIFTSIDE

Pav.

Cricket Ground

Drift Farm

Drift House

BLACKFORDBY

Moira Prim. Sch.

3

Clay Pit

29

Works

ROAD

HILL

COTTAGE

GORSE

Rawdon Villas

Hanging Hill

Swadlincote

Hanginghill Farm

LANE

RAWDON

Norris Hill

CORONATION

NORRIS

NORRIS HILL

E.M. GRO

ASHFIELD

CHERRY ROWN

TREE CL

WOODL

AMES

CEDAR

PINE

HOPPE CL

SYCAMORE

ASHFIELD

TANDY AV.

Chest Farm

4

Orchard View

SPRINGFIELD

MILLENNIUM

Conkers

MARQUIS

ORD

MARQUIS CT.

Maybury Wood

Works

Factory

Community Centre

SWEETHILL

HARTLEY

GRO

TOM CL

MARIS

SWEETHILL CL.

Sweethill Lodge

Sweethill Oak

CHESTNUT CL

Dilworth

WILLESLEY

5

HACKET

BATH LANE

Conkers Waterside

Sarah's Wood

Ashby-de-la-Zouch Canal

BATH

YD

ROMAN

VIA

DEVANA

FOREST LEA

STATION DR.

Office

ROAD

MEASHAM

Newfields

Newfield Farm

Football Ground

NEWFIELD

NEW ROW

BEEHIVE

BROOK

LODGE CL

PENN

ALVAN

DAYBELL

AV.

BRAMA

TAYLOR

REDGAR RD.

DE LA ZYTHN

Spoil Heap

WAY

MOIRA

ROAD

6

NORTH

WEST

SOUTH

LEICESTERSHIRE

DERBYSHIRE

Blencathra

AGOONA PARK

Hooborough

Football Ground

Brooklands Farm

3.15

Short Heath

NORTH

HEATH

SHORT

DONISTHORPE

PARK

Cricket Grd

Pav Club

Bowl. Playing Grn.

Fld.

Mem.

FURNACE

LA.

Furnace Plantation

Moira Furnace Museum

MEASHAM

IVANHOE

FURNACE LANE INDUSTRIAL ESTATE

Warren House Farm

Pav. Recreation Grd.

Chapel Houses

Fox Covert

Spoil Heap

Bramborough Farm

7

Short Heath

Shortheath Farm

LANE

HILL

SHORT

POPLAR AV.

Springfield Farm

Brook

Settling Tanks

Depot

SCHOOL ST.

DONISTHORPE WOODLAND PARK

ROAD

MOIRA

ASH

A   **B**   **36**   **C**   **D**   **E**

Hooborough

DONISTHORPE

Sewage Works

FINNEY CL.

JUBILEE TER.

3.11

DANK LA.

BUTTERCUP

GREENSIDE

VIOLET

COWSLIP

Comm. Cen.

32

DICKON

Donisthorpe Prim. Sch.

Bramb

ANNWELL PLACE

Annwell House

ANNWELL PLACE

Blackfordby Hall

Lady Wood

INGLES HILL CARAVAN SITE

Ingles Hill Farm

IVANHOE BUSINESS PARK

IVANHOE INDUSTRIAL ESTATE

Works

Dairy

Rosecrea

Newlands

Prestop Park Farm

Blackfordby Fields

Lynwood

Thorntop

Ingle Bank

Prestop Park

Holywell Spring Farm

Ingle's Hill

Playing Field

Cheatle's Barn

Lower Mead House

Shellbrook Farm

Shellbrook

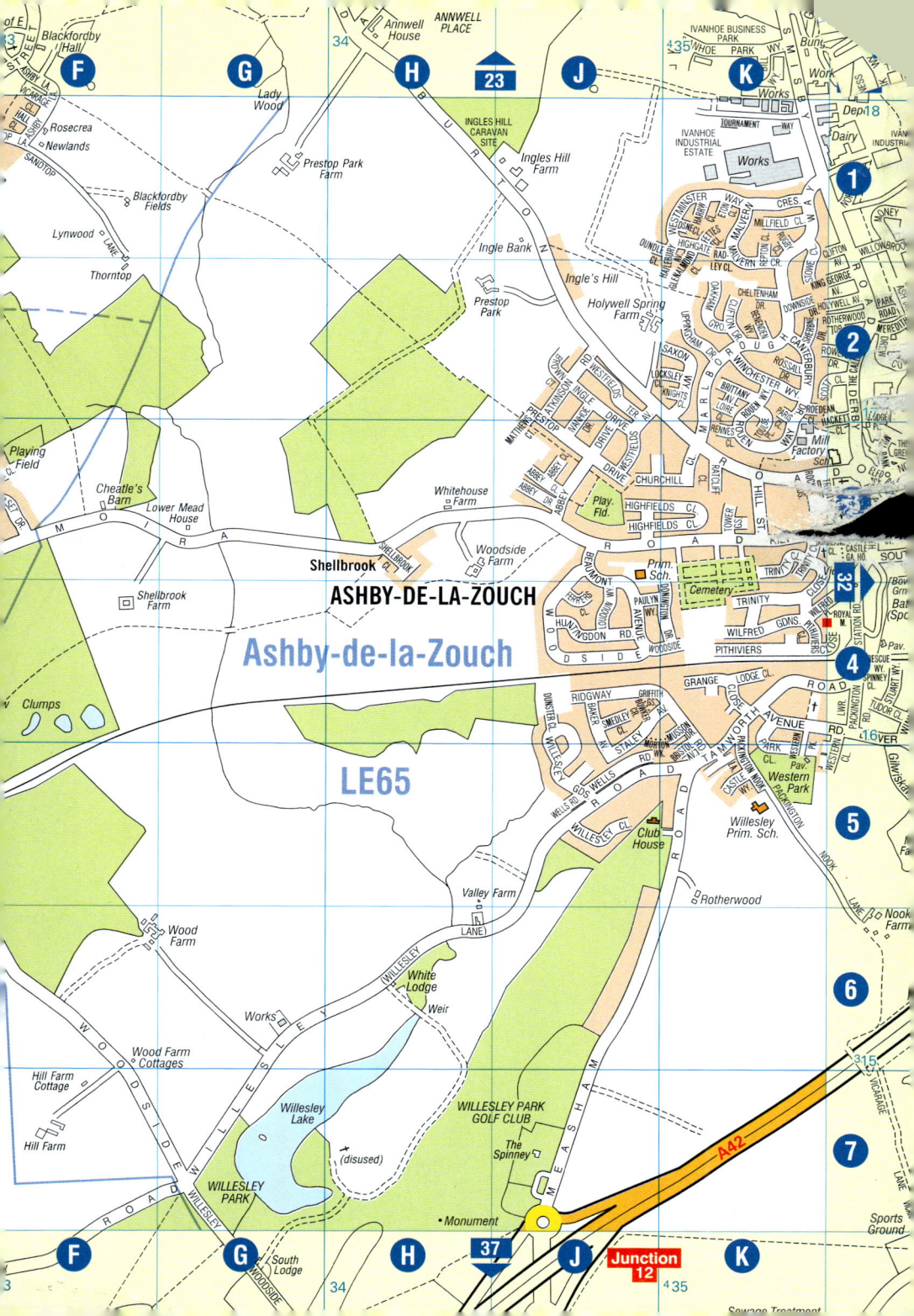

ASHBY-DE-LA-ZOUCH

Ashby-de-la-Zouch

LE65

Whitehouse Farm

Woodside Farm

Prim. Sch.

Cemetery

Clumps

Ridgway

Grange

Western Park

Willesley Prim. Sch.

Club House

Rotherwood

Valley Farm

LANE

Wood Farm

White Lodge

Weir

Works

Wood Farm Cottages

Hill Farm Cottage

Hill Farm

Willesley Lake

(disused)

WILLESLEY PARK

WILLESLEY PARK GOLF CLUB

The Spinney

Monument

South Lodge

Junction 12

A42

Nook Farm

Sports Ground

Sewage Treatment

32

A B C D E

36 37

The Bungalow
CLAYTONTHORPE
Depot
Dairy
Ivanhoe INDUSTRIAL ESTATE
Moneyhill Farm
Lawn Barn
MONEY HILL
Fox Covert
ASHBY-DE-LA-ZOUCH BY-PASS
DISCOVERY WY.
A511
Sports Field
B587
A42
ROAD

SMISBY
WAY
CRES.
18
MILLFIELD CL.
NORTHFIELDS
MONEY HILL
MONEY HILL
WILLOWBROOK
WOODCOTE
CLIFTON
KING GEORGE
Woodcote Prim. Sch.
Factory
Superstore
Flagstaff 42 BUSINESS PARK
Factory
NOTTINGHAM
Depot
Manor Ash Farm
Factory
RESOLUTION
PLANT WAY
ASTLEY WY.

1
DOWNSIDE
PARK ROAD
ASTUR DR.
ROTHERWOOD
HOLYWELL LA.
MEREDITH
DRY
Hood Park
Hood Park Leisure Cen.
Ivanhoe College
IVANHOE
NOTTINGHAM
STREET
ROAD
Factory Nottingham RD. INDUSTRIAL ESTATE
OAK CRESCENT
BIRCH RD.
ELM AV.
BEECH
SYCAMORE
EXCELSIOR
Wks.
Ashby PARK
CHARTER POINT WY.
A512
LOUNTSIDE
Junction 13
A511

2
ROWENA
ST. DAVIDS
RD.
ROSSALL WY.
ASBURY
HACKETT
ROEDEAN
Mill Factory
Factory
BRIDGE PL.
Museum
Lewis Charlton Sch.
Hood Park
Lib.
THE GREEN
NORTH STREET
HUNTINGTON
CT. LA.
Thtre.
Ashby Sch.
RANGE ROAD
Pav.
Playing Field
H ASHBY & DISTRICT HOSPITAL
SELINA
Manor Ho. Sch.
Ashby Sch.
Playing Field
Works
PENZ
2ND RD.
DUNBAR
LEITH
ABBOTS RD.
WAY
SMITHY
COALFIELD

ASHBY-DE-LA-ZOUCH

17
BURTON ROAD
MARKET
STREET
ELFORD
CLAIRDE
LOUDOUN DR.
LOUDOUN PL.
Mkt.
Store
Offs.
P
Ashby Castle (remains)
PRIOR PARK
MANOR RD.
Playing Field
LEICESTER
ROAD
PRIORFIELDS

31
TRINITY
VIC. CL.
WILFRED ST.
ROYAL
CLOSE
RESCUE WY.
SPINNEY CL.
STUART WY.
Bowl. Grns.
Bath Grounds (Sports Ground)
Cricket Ground
Pav.
PRIOR PARK
BELVOIR DR.
WARWICK
BAMBURS
ST. MICHAEL'S
PACKINGTON WAY
PRIOR PK.
THE CROFT
Works
PENN
DUNBAR
MELROSE
HARROTS
PRIORS RD.
EMMERDALE AV.
WINCHMILL CT.
CHES.
CONEY STEW

4
TAMWORTH
AVENUE
16
PARK CL.
WESTERN
Western Park
NOOK
LWR. PACKINGTON RD.
TUDOR DR.
WINDSOR
CAMBRIAN
MENDIP CL.
BRENDON
COTSWOLD WY.
WREKIN CL.
CHILTERN RSE.
HASTINGS WY.
ALTON WY.
WINDERMERE
ULLESWATER
AVENUE
Works
Cornworthy
CORKSCREW
LEICESTER
ROAD
LANE

5
GILMORLEAW
PACKINGTON ROAD
PEN
UPPER PACKINGTON ROAD
THE GABLES
Tollgate Cottage
Mill Farm
Sports Ground
CHAPMANS DYKE
Nook Farm
Breach Farm
Breach Hill

6
A42
Beech House
PACKINGTON ROAD
NORTON
Ashby-de-la-zouch
LE65
Barleydown Farm
Roecliffe Farm

315
A42

7
PACKINGTON
The Mill
VICARAGE
HALL LA.
HOMECROFT DR.
MILL STREET
NETHERCROFT DR.
ASHBY STREET
THE GRANGE
HEATHER LA.
BRIDGE ST.
38
NORTON LANE
SPRING LANE
Poultry Houses
Packington House
The Coach House
The Bungalow
The Rowans

Sports Ground
Manor Farm
Sch.

A B C D E
36 37

Sewage Treatment

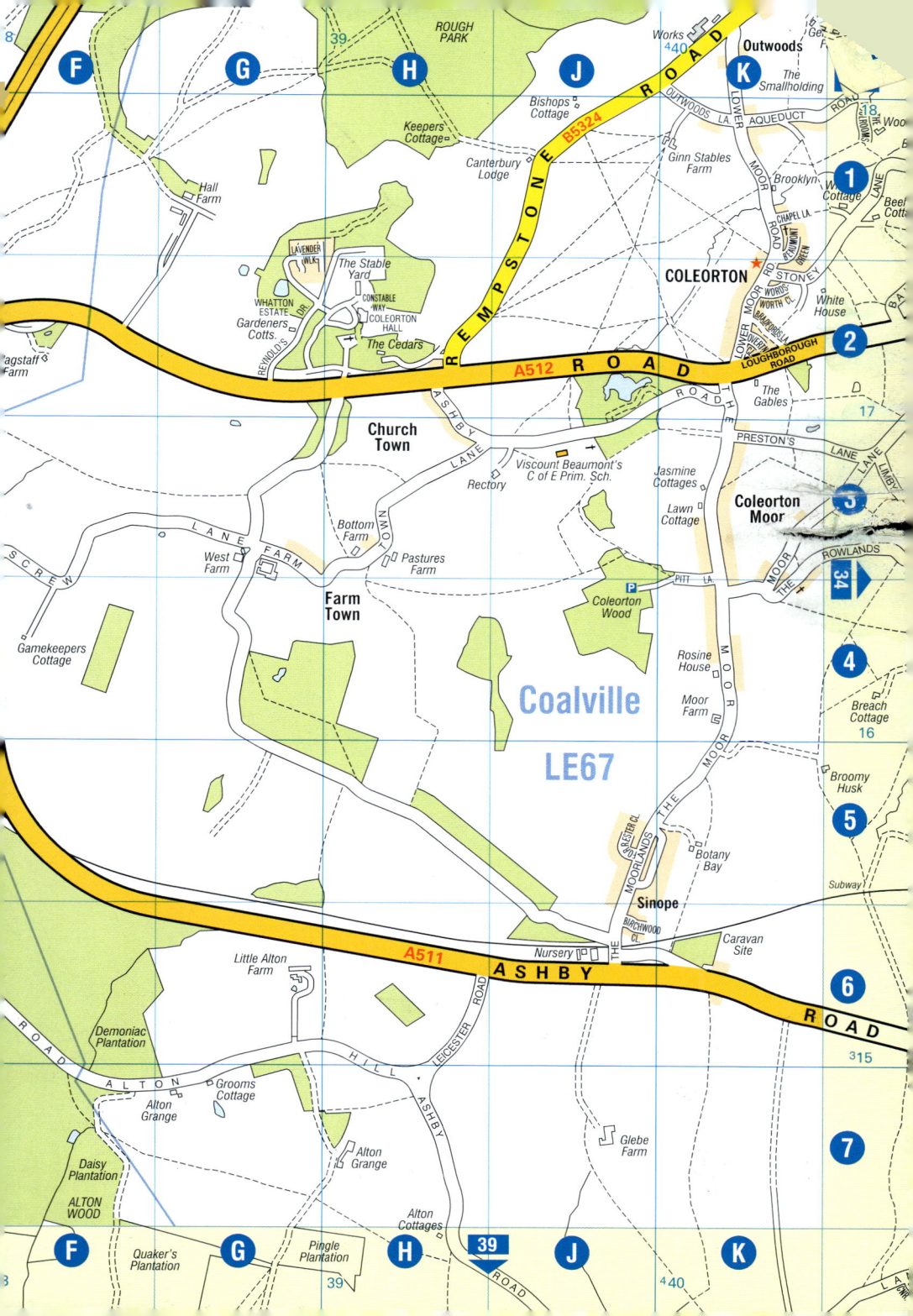

ROUGH PARK

39

F **G** **H** **J** Works **K** Outwoods

440

The Smallholding

Bishops Cottage

B5324

OUTWOODS LA.

LOWER AQUEDUCT

THE BROOMS

18.

Woo

Keepers Cottage

Canterbury Lodge

Ginn Stables Farm

MOOR ROAD

Brooklyn

CHAPEL LA.

Cottage

1

Beel Cott

LANE

Hall Farm

LAVENDER WLK

The Stable Yard

CONSTABLE WAY

COLEORTON HALL

WHATTON ESTATE

Gardeners Cotts.

REYNOLD'S DR.

The Cedars

COLEORTON

STONEY

PIEDMONT GREEN

White House

LOWER MOOR RD

WORTH CL.

BRADMOOR LA.

LOUGHBOROUGH ROAD

2

agstaff Farm

A512 ROAD

ROAD

The Gables

17

ASHBY LANE

Church Town

Rectory

Viscount Beaumont's C of E Prim. Sch.

Jasmine Cottages

PRESTON'S LANE

LANE

LIMBY

Coleorton Moor

3

SCREW

LANE

FARM

Bottom Farm

FARM TOWN

West Farm

Pastures Farm

Lawn Cottage

PITT LA.

ROWLANDS

34

Farm Town

Coleorton Wood

P

Rosine House

THE MOOR

4

Gamekeepers Cottage

Moor Farm

Breach Cottage

16

Coalville

Broomy Husk

5

THE MOORLANDS

CHESTER CL.

Botany Bay

Subway

LE67

BIRCHWOOD CL.

Sinope

THE

Caravan Site

6

ALTON ROAD

Little Alton Farm

HILL

LEICESTER ROAD

ASHBY

Nursery

THE

A511 ASHBY

ROAD

315

Demoniac Plantation

ALTON

Grooms Cottage

Alton Grange

Alton Grange

Glebe Farm

7

Daisy Plantation

ALTON WOOD

Quaker's Plantation

Pingle Plantation

Alton Cottages

39

ASHBY ROAD

440

F **G** **H** 39 **J** **K**

8

39

34

COLEORTON

Gelsmoor Farm · Bowl Grn · Clubhouse · The Poplars · Rose Cott. · Works · Hill Ho. · Field House Farm · Cinder Hill · Thringstone Prim Sch · Play. Fld. · Old Bakery

A · B · C · D · E

ASHBY ROAD · **ASHBY** · A512

Woolrooms · Brookdale · Miners' Institute · Peggs Green · Mill Farm · Millhouse Estate · Glebe · Henson's · Rec. Grd. Football Grd.

Willow Cottage · Beehive Cottage · Rec. Grd. · Anchor Farm · Lawn Villa · California Cottage · Clover Pl · Johnson Cl · Phoenix Bury Wk · Eldon Cl · Booth · Badgers Cft

1

White House · The Gables · Chapel La · Stoney · Worth Rd · Bakewells · Highfield House · Swannington Common · Talbot House Farm · John St · Hudson · Swallow Dale · Melrose · Swan Cl · Grace

LOUGHBOROUGH · A512

2

Swannington Windmill · Church · Hospital · Pumping Station · Redhill Bungalow · Comm. Cen. · Whitwick · MOOR

Preston's La

3

33 · The · Rowlands · Limby Hall · Redhill Farm · RED HILL · School Lane Farm · Martin · Cooper Wy · Valley Wy · Smith Ct.

Coalville

LE67

4

Limby Hall · Breach Cottage · Cuckoo Gap Farm · Brookside · Swannington C of E Prim. Sch. · Hall · Tan Yard · **Swannington** · Waverley House · **New Swannington** · Field Robinson Cl · Robinson

16

Broomy Husk · Willow Tree Farm · Deepdale · Swannington Incline · New Swannington Prim. Sch. · Thomas

5

Subway · Caravan Site · Stephenson College (Stephenson Studio Sch.) · **Thornborough** · Thornborough Bridle · Hermitage Golf Course

6

ASHBY · A511 · **ROAD** · **STEPHENSON**

Hoo Ash Farm · Phoenix Park · Brunel · Wylam Cl · Stephenson Ind. Est. · Stephenson Ct. · Martins Ct · Comm. Cen. · Coalville Bus. Cen. · Factory · Samson Cl · Atlas Cl · Vulcan Cl · White Business

3,15

SWANNINGTON RD · A447

All Saints C of E Prim. Sch. · **COALVILLE** · THE HERMITAGE INDUSTRIAL ESTATE · Works · Comet · Hector · Whitwick

7

Industrial Estate · Snibston Country Park · The Century Theatre · Bus Depot · Snibston · Hall · Factory Refuse Site · Market · Baker St · Office · High St · Library · Council · Bowl. Grn. · Park

40

A · B · C · D · E

41 · 42

ROAD
ASHBY RD.
44

F G H J K

Ashby Lodge
Cricket Grd.
Springfield
Play. Fld.

The Manor Farm
Grace Dieu Manor Sch.
Playing Field

Grace Dieu Lodge
Grace Dieu Hill

Woodyton Farm

Spring Burrow Lodge

18
SANDHOLE

NORTH WEST LEICESTERSHIRE
CHARNWOOD

Boat Ho.
The Hermitage
BLACKBROOK RESERVOIR

1

GRACE DIEU WOOD
Grace Dieu Park
Grace Dieu Warren
Warren Lodge
Grace Dieu Warren

Poachers Corner

LANE

THRINGSTONE

Hob's Hole
WARREN ROAD

Swannymote Farm

Strawberry Hill Plantation

2

17

Calvary Rock
Twentysteps
Turry Log Farm
Carr Hill Rock
Grimley's Rock
Saddle House
Temple Hill
Broad Hill

CADEMAN WOOD

High Cademan
Picnic Site

Swannymote Rock

High Sharpley

SWANNYMOTE

Gun Hill
Gunhill Rough

Drybrook Lodge Farm
Drybrook Wood

3

LOUGHBOROUGH ROAD
OAKS

Bleak House
St. Catherine Villa

Dry BROOK

ROAD

Prim. Sch.
Holy Cross Sch.
Motte & Bailey
CASTLE HILL

WHITWICK

The Tower House
Vicarage Forest Farm
Ratchet Hill

Football Ground

4

16

Whitwick Cemetery
Hermitage Leisure Centre
Playing Fields
Pav. & Club Ho.
Ground
Play Area

BEAUMONT
ST BERNARDS

Whitwick Quarry

LEICESTER ROAD

5

Hillside Cottage

Weir

6

Forest View

THE PINGS
TRESSALL

Glebe Farm

Coalville Rugby Football Club
Rec. Ground
Pav.

WARREN HILLS
315
Sports Hall
Castle Rock High School
King Edward VII Science & Sport College
Games Court
Forest Way School
Sch.

7

A511
WAY
A511

WILLOW GN
OAKHAM

COALVILLE COMMUNITY HOSPITAL

F G H J K

41
45

Cemetery
GREENACRES

Agar Nook
BLACKWOOD

Cricket

F G H J K

36

A   **B**   **C**   **D**   **E**

31   32

Springfield Farm

Brook

Settling

Depot

POPLAR

IVANHOE

STHORPE WOODLAND PARK

30

FINNEY CL.
JUBILEE TER.
PLUMTREE COTTS.
GREENSIDE
CL. THE GREEN

DAWKINS

BUTTERCUP

VIOLET

DAISY

BELL CL.

FOXGLOVE

Comm. Cen.

Donisthorpe Prim. Sch.

Bambro Farm

Redholme Farm

SEALS RD.
NEW ST.
CHAPEL STREET

BARKLAM CL.

THE PETERLEAS

Bowl Grn.

Cricket Grd.

Pav.

Cemetery

Playing Field

DONISTHORPE

314

Hobday Hills Plantation

NARROW LA.
HOLLY CL.
TALBOT PL.
IVY
TALBOT PL.

†

The Grange

Vicarage

RAMSCLIFF

BASKING AVENUE

Playing Field Comm. Cen.

Cockspur Bridge

ASHBY ROAD

STREET

MEASHAM

MOIRA

Playing Field

Lakeside

Lowlands Bungalow

Lowlands Farm

The Hawthorns

Hall Farm

Donisthorpe Hall

Saltersford Valley Local Nature Reserve

Steam Mill Bridge

PASTURES

Playing Field

Oakthorpe Sports & Leisure Centre

Acresford Plantation

ACRESFORD ROAD

HALL LANE

Saltersford Brook

Oakthorpe Prim. Sch.

House Farm

Oakthorpe

BODKIN ROW

2

3

13

Stanleigh Plantation

BONDGATE
MAIN ST.
THE SQUARE
SILVER ST.
NEW SCHOOL ST.

STREET

4

MEASHAM

Willowbeds

Saltersford Cottages

Saltersford Bridge

Saltersford Farm

River Mease

Sewage Works

CORONATION

CHAPEL ROAD

Oak Villa

STRETTON VW.
LANE
THE STREET

Springfield Farm

Swadlincote DE12

A42

5

12

Hall Farm

Stretton en le Field

Stretton House

RECTORY
LANE

BURTON ROAD

REPTON

HUNTINGDON

HUNTINGDON CT.

Sewage Works

DYSON'S CLOSE

WESTMINSTER INDUSTRIAL ESTATE

THE CROC

6

RIVERSIDE COURT

Side Hollows Farm

River Mease

WAY

MALLARD
WIGEON
WORDSWORTH
BARNES

7

11

A42

Quarry Plantation

Ashlea Cottage

Birds' Hill

Manor House Farm

TAMWORTH

MEASHAM RD.

White House

A   **B**   **C**   **D**   **E**

31   32

A444

37
Hill Farm
(disused)
The Spinney
MEASHAM RD.
Monument
WILLESLEY PARK
Junction 12
31
38
A42
Ashby-de-la-Zouch
LE65
Sewage Treatment Works
South Lodge
Saltersford Brook
WOODSIDE
WILLESLEY
Sweethill Cottage
Park Farm
MEASHAM RD.
B4116
MEASHAM
Reservoir (covered)
Brickfield Plantation
Pasture Farm
LANE
Field Farm Cottages
Field Farm
NORTH WLK.
Emscote
The Firs
Champney Springs (Health Resort)
Arlick Farm
ASHBY ROAD
GRASSY LANE
Measham House Cottage
Measham House Farm
Nursery
Fields Farm
Nature Park
LEICESTER ROAD
WOODFIELD COTTS.
GREENFIELD RD.
Sch.
BOSWORTH ROAD
SWEPSTONE ROAD
Measham Leis. Cen.
Library
Measham Mus.
Prim. Sch.
Recreation Ground
Cemetery
MEASHAM
The Bungalow
Measham Hall
Stanhope House
Measham Fields Farm
Ivyleigh
Depot
Measham Lodge
Works
Coronet House
Clay Pit
Brook
Gilwiskaw
Bosworth Grange
GALLOWS LANE
HIGH STREET
ATHERSTONE ROAD
BABELAKE STREET
HORSES LANE
IBSTOCK COTTAGES
CRESCENT
Sports Ground
Bowl. Grn.

A B 32 C D E

Houses
Packington House
The Bungalow

Manor Farm
MILL STREET
HALL
36
NETHERCROFT DR.
LITTLE
NETHERCROFT DR.
Sch.
BRIDGE HEATHER
St.
BROOK CL.
PACKINGTON
The Coach House
37

The Rowans

1
Sewage Treatment Works
Sports Ground
ROAD

Barn Farm
HEATHER LA.

Hill Farm
Hill Farm

314

Ashby-de-la-Zouch

MEASHAM

Yew Tree Farm

2
Weir
Redburrow Farm
LE65

BABELAKE

Lowerfield Farm

ROAD ASHBY

3
GL WISKAW
Stonehouse Farm

REDBURROW

13
37
STREET

4
Arlick Farm

Normanton Lodge Farm

Normanton le Heath

ROAD HE

SCH

LANE

HIGHFIELDS CL.
MAIN STREET
THE HOLLOW
Potwell Farm

Hillcrest
Manor Farm

5

12
Measham Hall

6
Stanhope House
Clock Mill
Mill Top House
SWEPSTONE

Odd Farm

Depot

7
Swadlincote
DE12

Tempe Farm

ASHBY LANE

Upperfields Farm

ROAD MAIN
Dishley Farm

Mount Pleasant

Dishley Grange
Park Corner
Swepstone
The Cottage
SWEPSTONE

11
Spring Cottage
STREET
JUBILEE CFT.
37

A B 36. C D E

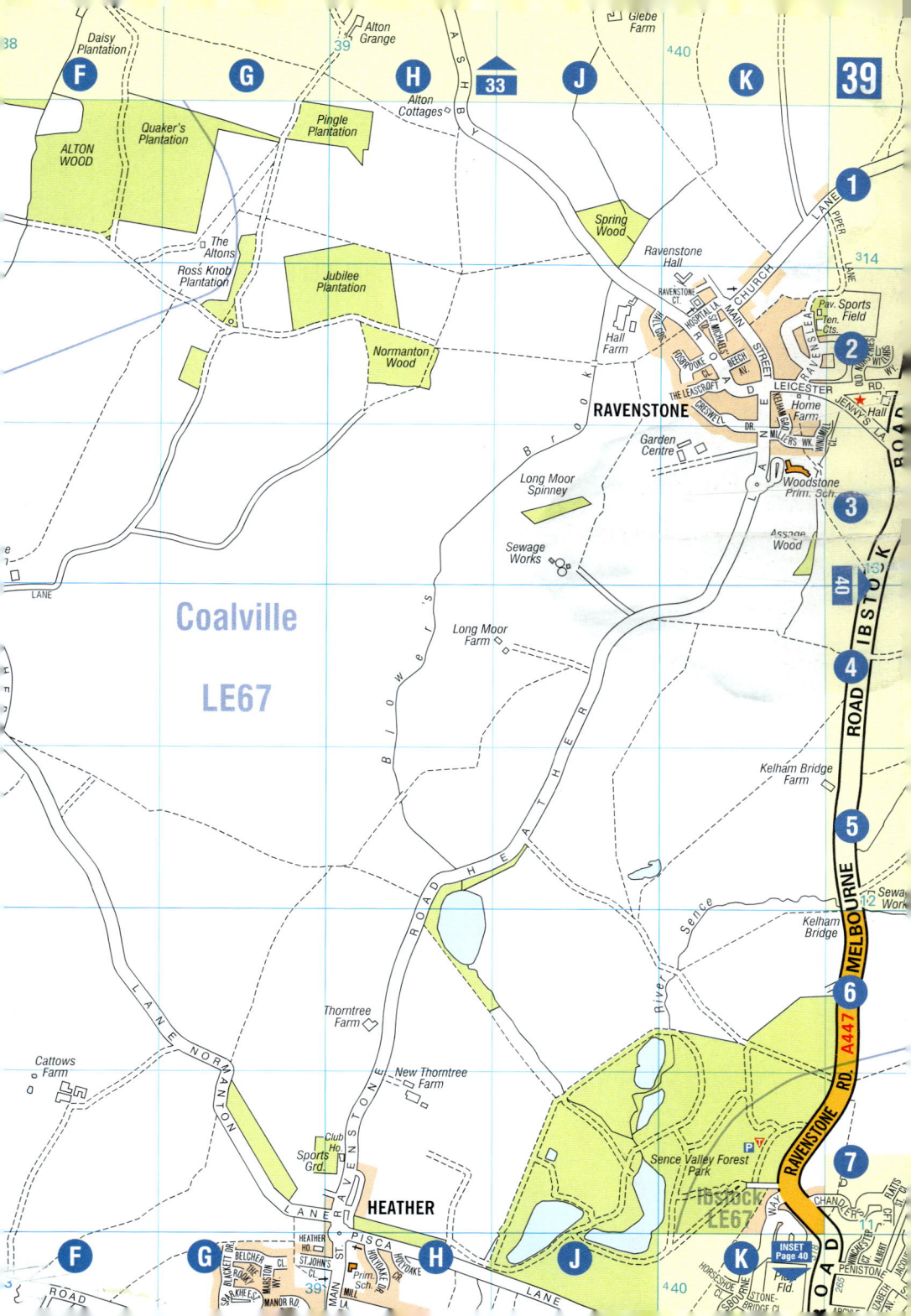

F **G** **H** **J** **K**

33

1

2

3

4

5

6

7

38

39

440

314

40

12

Daisy Plantation

Alton Grange

Glebe Farm

Alton Cottages

Quaker's Plantation

ALTON WOOD

Pingle Plantation

Spring Wood

Ravenstone Hall

The Altons

Ross Knob Plantation

Jubilee Plantation

Normanton Wood

Ravenstone Ct.

Hall Farm

HOSPITAL LA

ST MICHAEL'S

FOSBROOKE

MAIN STREET

CHURCH STREET

RAVENSLEA

OLD MANOR RD

WITHERS

PIPER LANE

LANE

Pav. Sports Ten. Field Cts.

Ravenstone

THE LEASCROFT

KELHAM ROAD

CRESWELL

LANE

LEICESTER RD.

Home Farm

JENNY'S LA.

Hall

MILLERS WK.

WINDMILL

BEECH AV.

DR.

CL.

Garden Centre

Woodstone Prim. Sch.

Long Moor Spinney

Assage Wood

Sewage Works

IBSTOCK ROAD

Brook

Long Moor Farm

Coalville

LE67

Kelham Bridge Farm

Sewa Work

Kelham Bridge

Sence River

HEATHER ROAD

LANE NORMANTON

Cattows Farm

Thorntree Farm

New Thorntree Farm

MELBOURNE

A447

RAVENSTONE RD.

Sence Valley Forest Park

IBSTOCK LE67

CHANDOS

Club Ho. Sports Grd.

RAVENSTONE LANE

HEATHER HO.

St JOHN'S CL.

BELCHER DR.

BLASKETT LA.

MARSTON WY.

MANOR RD.

MAIN ST.

PISCA LANE

Prim. Sch.

MILL LA.

HILLDALE CR.

HISTOKE CR.

HEATHER

ALBERT

PENISTONE

HORSESHOE CL.

STONE BRIDGE CL.

WALK

CHANDOS CFT.

Rec. Fld.

INSET Page 40

440

39

F **G** **H** **J** **K**

ROAD

ROAD

40

COALVILLE

INSET

Ibstock LE67

IBSTOCK

ELLISTOWN

Donington le Heath

Hugglescote

Snibston

Ravenstone

Snibston Country Park

Coalville Town FC

Discovery Driving Range & Golf Centre

Grange Nature Reserve

Fishing Lakes

The Century Theatre

Snibston

Coalville Business Pk.

The Belvoir Shop. Cen.

Belvoirdale Prim. Sch.

Coalville Central

The Piggeries

Standard Road

Highfield

Forest Road

Grange Road

Hugglescote Prim. Sch.

Recreation Ground

Manor Ho. & Gdns

Donington le Heath

Smiths Farm

Berryhills Farm

Kelham Bridge Farm

Woodstone

Jenny's La.

Home Farm

Leicester Road

St. Mary's Lane

Grange Farm

Pav. Sports Field

Whitegates Farm

Coach Park

Oaks Industrial Estate

Colliery

Railway

The Courtyard

The Hermitage Industrial Estate

Works

Factory Refuse Site

Bus Depot

Council Offices

Sence Valley Forest Park

Coalville LE67

Clay Pit

Ibstock Industrial Estate

Cricket Ground

Ibstock Welfare

Bowling Grn.

Works

Cemetery

Redlands Estate

Victoria

Wellington

Brookfield Farm

Jun. & Inf. Schs.

Sports Grd.

Play. Fld.

Comm. Coll.

Lib.

Redholme Bungalow Farm

Poplar Farm

Clare Fm.

Valley Farm

Playground

Sports Ground

The Elms

The Limes

Leicester Road

Whiten Road

South Street

MELBOURNE ROAD A447

LANE SWANNINGTON RD.

ROAD WASH

IBSTOCK ROAD

ASHBY ROAD

STATION ROAD

MIDLAND

RAVENSTONE RD.

A447

Coalville

LE67

Forest Way School

Coalville Rugby Football Club

Coalville Community Hospital

Broomleys Farm

Broomleys Sch.

Greenhill

Agar Nook

Cemetery

Greenacres

Cricket Ground

Sports Field

Forest Way School

Bardon Hill Sports Club

Sports Ground

Bardon Hill Quarry

Bardon

Bardon House

Works

Bardon Hill

Louella Stud

Grange Farm Bus. Pk.

Upper Grange Farm

Upper Grange Farm

Glebe Farm

Whitwick Bus. Pk.

Coalville Park

Tennis Cts.

Scotlands Ind. Est.

Playing Fields

Bowling Green

Playing Field

Lodge

Maple Ct.

Cartwright

Cedar Ct.

Forest Business Park

Pine Ct.

Hilltop Industrial Estate

Ash Ct.

Beveridge La.

Bardon 22 Industrial Park

Cliffe Hill Rail Terminal

Interlink Park

Interlink Way West Interlink

Bardon Business Park

Works

Little Battleflats Farm

Reservoir

Coal Yard

South Leicester Industrial Estate

St. Christophers Park

Battleflat Lodge Farm

Battle Flat

Cliffe Hill Quarry

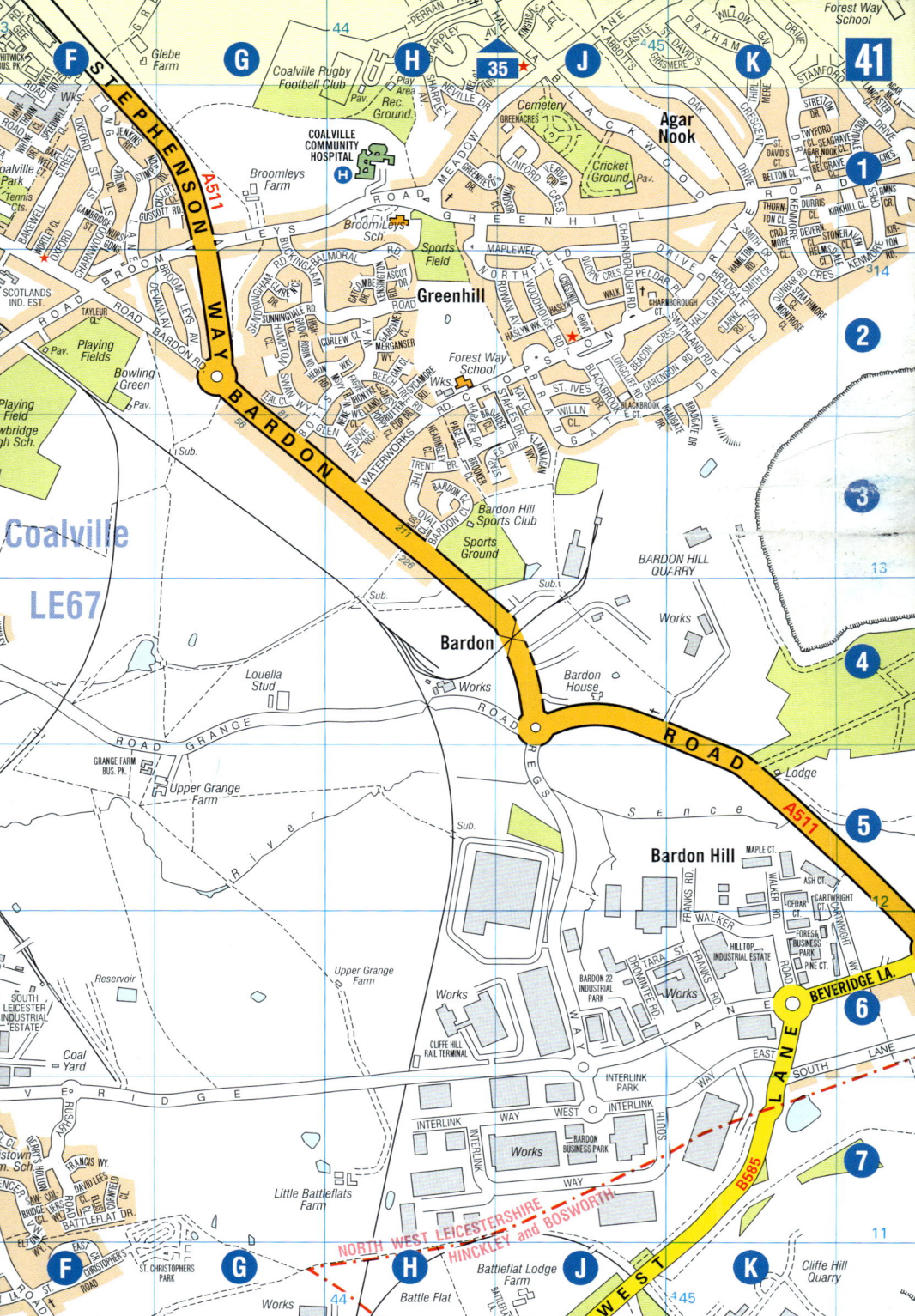

NORTH WEST LEICESTERSHIRE
HINCKLEY and BOSWORTH

WEST

STEPHENSON WAY

BARDON

ROAD

A511

B585

LANE

SOUTH

EAST

RUSHEY

BRIDGE

River Sence

A511

A511

35

45

44

44

45

13

314

13

11

12

F G H J K

F G H J K

1 2 3 4 5 6 7

INDEX

Including Streets, Places & Areas, Hospitals etc., Industrial Estates,
Selected Flats & Walkways, Stations and Selected Places of Interest.

HOW TO USE THIS INDEX

1. Each street name is followed by its Postcode District, then by its Locality abbreviation(s) and then by its map reference;
e.g. **Abbey Dr.** LE65: Ash Z . . . .3J **31** is in the LE65 Postcode District and the Ashby-de-la-Zouch Locality and is to be found in square 3J on page **31**.
The page number is shown in bold type.

2. A strict alphabetical order is followed in which Av., Rd., St., etc. (though abbreviated) are read in full and as part of the street name;
e.g. **Ash La.** appears after **Ashland Dr.** but before **Ashlar Dr.**

3. Streets and a selection of flats and walkways that cannot be shown on the mapping, appear in the index with the thoroughfare to which they are connected shown in brackets; e.g. **Albion Ter.** *DE14: Bur T* . . . .1K **13** (off Derby Rd.)

4. Addresses that are in more than one part are referred to as not continuous.

5. Places and areas are shown in the index in BLUE TYPE and the map reference is to the actual map square in which the town centre or area is located and not to the place name shown on the map; e.g. ANSLOW 7B **8**

6. An example of a selected place of interest is **Ashby-de-la-Zouch Mus.** 3A **32**

7. An example of a station is **Burton-on-Trent Station (Rail)** 4H **13**

8. An example of a Hospital, Hospice or selected Healthcare facility is **ASHBY & DISTRICT HOSPITAL** 3B **32**

GENERAL ABBREVIATIONS

App. : Approach	**Gdns.** : Gardens	**Pk.** : Park
Arc. : Arcade	**Gth.** : Garth	**Pas.** : Passage
Av. : Avenue	**Ga.** : Gate	**Pl.** : Place
Bri. : Bridge	**Grn.** : Green	**Ri.** : Rise
Bldgs. : Buildings	**Gro.** : Grove	**Rd.** : Road
Bus. : Business	**Hgts.** : Heights	**Rdbt.** : Roundabout
Cen. : Centre	**Ho.** : House	**Shop.** : Shopping
Cl. : Close	**Ho's.** : Houses	**Sth.** : South
Cnr. : Corner	**Ind.** : Industrial	**Sq.** : Square
Cott. : Cottage	**Info.** : Information	**St.** : Street
Cotts. : Cottages	**La.** : Lane	**Ter.** : Terrace
Ct. : Court	**Lit.** : Little	**Trad.** : Trading
Cres. : Crescent	**Lwr.** : Lower	**Up.** : Upper
Cft. : Croft	**Mnr.** : Manor	**Va.** : Vale
Dr. : Drive	**Mdw.** : Meadow	**Vw.** : View
E. : East	**Mdws.** : Meadows	**Vs.** : Villas
Ent. : Enterprise	**M.** : Mews	**Vis.** : Visitors
Est. : Estate	**Mt.** : Mount	**Wlk.** : Walk
Fld. : Field	**Mus.** : Museum	**W.** : West
Flds. : Fields	**Nth.** : North	**Yd.** : Yard

LOCALITY ABBREVIATIONS

Acre : **Acresford**	Ell : **Ellistown**	Ros : **Rosliston**
Alb V : **Albert Village**	Etw : **Etwall**	Scro : **Scropton**
Alre : **Alrewas**	Fin : **Findern**	Shep : **Shepshed**
Ans : **Anslow**	Fos : **Foston**	Sho H : **Short Heath**
App M : **Appleby Magna**	Frad : **Fradley**	Smis : **Smisby**
Ash Z : **Ashby-de-la-Zouch**	Hart : **Hartshorne**	Snar : **Snarestone**
Bar H : **Bardon Hill**	Hatt : **Hatton**	Stan : **Stanton**
Bar N : **Barton-under-Needwood**	Hea : **Heather**	Stap : **Stapenhill**
Blac : **Blackfordby**	Hilt : **Hilton**	Stre : **Stretton**
Boo : **Boothorpe**	Hug : **Hugglescote**	Stre F : **Stretton en le Field**
Bou : **Boundary**	Ibs : **Ibstock**	Swad : **Swadlincote**
Bran : **Branston**	Lin : **Linton**	Swan : **Swannington**
Bret : **Bretby**	Lou : **Lount**	Swep : **Swepstone**
Burn : **Burnaston**	Mea : **Measham**	Tate : **Tatenhill**
Bur T : **Burton-on-Trent**	Mid : **Midway**	Thri : **Thringstone**
Cald : **Caldwell**	Moi : **Moira**	Tick : **Ticknall**
Calke : **Calke**	Neth : **Netherseal**	Tut : **Tutbury**
Cas G : **Castle Gresley**	New : **Newhall**	Wal T : **Walton-on-Trent**
Chu G : **Church Gresley**	New S : **Newton Solney**	Whit : **Whitwick**
Coal : **Coalville**	Nor H : **Normanton le Heath**	W'ley : **Willesley**
Cole : **Coleorton**	Oak : **Oakthorpe**	W'ton : **Willington**
Cot E : **Coton in the Elms**	Ove : **Overseal**	Win : **Winshill**
Don H : **Donington le Heath**	Pac : **Packington**	Wood : **Woodville**
Don : **Donisthorpe**	Ran : **Rangemore**	Wych : **Wychnor**
Drak : **Drakelow**	Rav : **Ravenstone**	Yox : **Yoxall**
Dun : **Dunstall**	Rep : **Repton**	
Egg : **Egginton**	Rol D : **Rolleston-on-Dove**	

A

Abbey, The DE65: Rep 4K **11**	**Abney Dr.** DE12: Mea 6F **37**	**Aire Cl.** DE65: Hilt 4A **6**
Abbey Arc. DE14: Bur T 5K **13**	**Abney Wlk.** DE12: Mea 6F **37**	**Albert Rd.** DE11: Chu G 6H **21**
Abbey Cl. LE65: Ash Z 3J **31**	**Acacia Av.** DE11: Mid 1J **21**	LE67: Coal 1E **40**
Abbey Dr. LE65: Ash Z 3J **31**	**Acresford Rd.** DE12: Acre, Don 3A **36**	**Albert St.** DE14: Bur T 3H **13**
Abbey Lodge Cl. DE11: New 1H **21**	DE12: Ove 7J **29**	LE67: Ibs 6B **40**
Abbey Rd. LE67: Coal 6K **35**	**Acresford Vw.** DE12: Ove 6J **29**	**ALBERT VILLAGE** 7K **21**
Abbey St. DE14: Bur T 6J **13**	**Adam Morris Way** LE67: Coal 2E **40**	**Albion Cl.** DE12: Moi 5D **30**
Abbot Cl. DE14: Bur T 4F **13**	**Adams Cl.** DE11: Hart 1D **22**	**Albion St.** DE11: Wood 6C **22**
Abbotsford Rd. LE65: Ash Z 4B **32**	**Adcock Rd.** LE67: Coal 6D **34**	**Albion Ter.** *DE14: Bur T* 1K **13**
Abbotts Cl. DE11: New 2H **21**	**Adcocks Yd.** DE12: Mea 5F **37**	(off Derby Rd.)
AGAR NOOK 1K **41**	**Addie Rd.** DE13: Bur T 1G **13**	**Alderbrook Cl.** DE13: Rol D 2G **9**
Abbott's Oak Dr. LE67: Coal 7J **35**	**Adelaide Cres.** DE15: Win 5D **14**	**Alder Gro.** DE15: Stap 1A **20**
Abbotts Rd. DE11: New 2H **21**	**Agar Nook Ct.** LE67: Coal 1K **41**	**Alderholme Dr.** DE13: Stre 5A **10**
Abbotts Cres. DE12: Mea 6F **37**	**Agar Nook La.** LE67: Coal 7K **35**	**ALDER MOOR** 3D **8**
	Aintree Cl. DE14: Bran 1E **18**	**Alders, The** DE13: Bar N 7F **17**
		Alders Brook DE65: Hilt 4J **5**

Aldersley Cl. DE65: Fin 4K 7
Alderson Dr. DE13: Stre 5A 10
Alders Reach DE13: Rol D 2G 9
Alexandra Ct. DE12: Ove 5J 29
   DE15: Win .4B 14
Alexandra Dr. DE13: Yox 1B 16
Alexandra Pas. DE11: Swad 5J 21
Alexandra Rd. DE11: Swad 5J 21
   DE12: Ove .5J 29
   DE15: Win .4B 14
Alfred St. DE14: Bur T 5H 13
Alice Gdns. DE12: Ove 5J 29
Alleyne Cl. DE11: Swad 5K 21
Allison Av. DE11: Swad 5J 21
Allison Cl. LE65: Ash Z 1A 32
All Saints Cl. LE67: Coal 7C 34
All Saints Cft. DE14: Bur T 7H 13
All Saints Rd. DE14: Bur T 6G 13
Alma Rd. DE11: New 2G 21
Alma St. DE14: Bur T 6H 13
Almond Ct. DE13: Stre 5K 9
Almond Gro. DE11: New 3H 21
Almshouses DE65: Etw 1C 6
ALREWAS 6D 24
Althorp Way DE13: Stre 6J 9
Alton Hill LE67: Rav 7F 33
Alton Way LE65: Ash Z 4B 32
Alwyn Rd. DE13: Yox 2B 16
Amber Ct. DE14: Bur T 4H 13
   (off Grants Yd.)
Amberlands DE13: Stre 5A 10
Amberwood DE11: New 3H 21
Amersham Way DE12: Mea 4E 36
Anchor Ct. DE11: Swad 4K 21
Anchor La. LE67: Cole 1B 34
Anderby Gdns. DE11: Chu G 6G 21
Anderstaff Ind. Est.
   DE14: Bur T 2K 13
Anglesey Bus. Pk. DE14: Bur T 5G 13
Anglesey Ct. DE14: Bur T 6G 13
Anglesey Moor Rd. DE14: Bur T 5H 13
Anglesey Rd. DE14: Bur T 6G 13
Anglesey St. DE14: Bur T 4E 12
Anglia Dr. DE11: Chu G 7G 21
Annwell La. LE65: Smis 7H 23
ANSLOW 7B 8
Anslow La. DE13: Bur T, Rol D 4F 9
Anslow Pk. Cotts. DE13: Ans 6C 8
Anson Ct. DE14: Bur T 4K 13
Anson Rd. DE13: Alre 7D 24
Appleby Glade DE11: Cas G 6E 20
Appleby Glade Ind. Est. DE11: Swad 6F 21
Appleton Cl. DE11: New 2G 21
   DE15: Stap 1K 19
Appletree Rd. DE65: Hatt 4B 4
APS Ind. Pk. DE14: Bur T 2K 13
Aqueduct Rd. LE67: Cole 1K 33
Arden Cl. DE13: Bar N 7G 17
Argyle St. LE67: Ibs 6B 40
Ariston Dr. DE11: Wood 7B 22
Armed Forces Memorial
   (National Memorial Arboretum) 7F 25
Armitage Hill DE13: Dun 4H 17
Arnold Cl. DE11: Cas G 2F 29
Arnside Cl. DE11: Chu G 7K 21
Arthur Rice DE11: New 3F 21
Arthurs Ct. DE13: Stre 4K 9
Arthur St. LE65: Ash Z 2F 29
   DE14: Bur T 2H 13
Ascot Cl. DE15: Win 4B 14
Ascot Dr. LE67: Coal 2H 41
Ascott Dr. DE11: New 1H 21
Ashbourne Dr. DE11: Cas G 7G 21
Ashbrook DE15: Stap 6B 14
Ashburton Rd. LE67: Hug 3C 40
ASHBY & DISTRICT HOSPITAL 3B 32
Ashby Castle (remains) 3B 32
ASHBY-DE-LA-ZOUCH 3A 32
Ashby-de-la-Zouch By-Pass DE11: Bou . . .6G 23
   LE65: Ash Z, Smis . . . . . . .6G 23 & 1C 32
Ashby-de-la-Zouch Mus. 3A 32
Ashby La. DE11: Blac 7F 23
   LE67: Swep 7C 38
Ashby Pk. LE65: Ash Z 3D 32
Ashby Rd. DE11: Bou, Wood 6D 22
   DE12: Don 1D 36
   DE12: Mea 4G 37
   DE12: Moi .5C 30
   DE15: Bret, Bur T, Win 4A 14
   LE65: Ash Z, Cole 2E 32
   LE65: Pac .7B 32
   LE67: Coal 6J 33
   LE67: Cole 2H 33
   LE67: Ibs .6A 40
   (not continuous)
   LE67: Nor H 3E 38
   LE67: Rav .2K 39
   LE67: Thri, Whit . . . . .1D 34 & 1H 35
Ashby Rd. E. DE15: Bret 6E 14

Ash Ct. LE67: Bar H 5K 41
Ash Dale LE67: Thri 2E 34
Ashdale Cl. DE11: Ibs 7A 40
Ashdale Cl. DE15: Stap 7B 14
Ash Dr. DE12: Mea 4F 37
   LE65: Ash Z 2A 32
Ashfield Dr. DE12: Moi 3E 30
Ashford Rd. DE13: Bur T 1F 13
   LE67: Whit 4E 34
Ashford Way DE11: Chu G 6G 21
Ash Gro. La. DE65: Egg 7D 6
Ashland Dr. LE67: Coal 7B 34
Ash La. DE65: Etw 1B 6
Ashlar Dr. DE12: Don 1C 36
Ashleigh Av. DE11: New 3G 21
Ashley Cl. DE12: Ove 6J 29
   DE15: Win .4B 14
Ashley Ct. DE15: Win 4B 14
Ashover Rd. DE11: New 3F 21
Ash St. DE14: Bur T 6G 13
Ashtree Cl. DE11: New 2G 21
Ash Tree Rd. DE13: Bar N 7F 17
   LE67: Hug .3C 40
Ash Vw. Cl. DE65: Etw 1C 6
Ashworth Av. DE15: Stap 5D 14
Askew Gro. DE65: Rep 4K 11
Aspen Cl. DE12: Mea 4F 37
   LE67: Rav .7B 34
Aspen M. DE15: Stap 2A 20
Aspen Rd. DE13: Bar N 1G 25
Aspens Hollow LE67: Thri 2E 34
Astbury Way DE11: Wood 7C 22
Astil St. DE15: Stap 6A 14
Astley Way LE65: Ash Z 2C 32
Aston Dr. DE11: New 1H 21
Astron Bus. Pk. DE11: Swad 5G 21
Atherstone Rd. DE12: Mea 6F 37
Athlestan Way DE13: Stre 4G 9
Atkinson Rd. LE65: Ash Z 2J 31
Atlas Ct. LE67: Coal 7E 34
Atlas Ho. LE67: Coal 1D 40
Atlas Rd. LE67: Coal 7E 34
Audens Way DE11: Mid 2K 21
Audley Cl. DE13: Alre 6D 24
Ault Dene DE11: Swad 4B 22
Aults Cl. DE65: Fin 4K 7
Avenue Rd. LE65: Ash Z 4K 31
   LE67: Coal 2E 40
Averham Cl. DE11: Swad 5H 21
Aviation La. DE13: Bur T 3B 12
Avon Cl. DE11: Swad 2J 21
Avon Way DE15: Stap 6B 14
   DE65: Hilt .5J 5

B

Babbington Cl. DE13: Tut 1B 8
Babelake St. LE65: Pac 2A 38
Back La. DE13: Yox 1A 16
   DE65: Hilt .3H 5
Badgers Cft. LE67: Thri 2E 34
Bailey Av. DE12: Ove 6H 29
Bailey St. DE14: Bur T 6J 13
Bakehouse Cl. LE67: Hug 3D 40
Baker Av. LE65: Ash Z 4J 31
Baker St. DE11: Chu G, Swad 5K 21
   (not continuous)
   DE15: Stap 1K 19
   LE67: Coal 7D 34
Bakery Ct. LE65: Ash Z 3A 32
Bakewell Cl. LE67: Coal 1F 41
Bakewell Grn. DE11: New 3F 21
Bakewells La. LE67: Cole 2A 34
Bakewell St. LE67: Coal 1F 41
Balata Way DE13: Stre 7J 9
Balfour St. DE13: Bur T 1H 13
Balk, The DE13: Tut 7C 4
Balmoral Gdns. DE15: Win 4B 14
Balmoral Rd. DE15: Win 4B 14
   LE67: Coal 2G 41
Baltimore Cl. DE11: New 1H 21
Bamborough Cl. DE13: Stre 7J 9
Bamburgh Cl. LE65: Ash Z 4A 32
Bancroft, The DE65: Etw 1C 6
Bancroft Cl. DE65: Hilt 3J 5
Bank Pas. DE11: Swad 5J 21
Bank St. DE11: Cas G 1H 29
Bank Wlk. DE13: Bur T 6G 9
Bannatyne's Health Club
   Burton upon Trent 7D 12
Barberry Cl. DE14: Bur T 5E 12
Bardolph Cl. DE11: Swad 5G 21
BARDON 4H 41
Bardon 22 Ind. Pk. LE67: Bar H 6J 41
Bardon Bus. Pk. LE67: Bar H 7J 41
Bardon Cl. LE67: Coal 7D 34
BARDON HILL 6K 41
Bardon Rd. LE67: Bar H, Coal 2G 41

Bargate La. DE65: W'ton 1J 11
Barker Round Way DE14: Bur T 1K 13
Barklam Cl. DE12: Don 1B 36
Bar La. DE13: Bar N 5C 16
Barley Cl. DE14: Bur T 1K 13
Barleycorn Cl. DE15: Stap 6B 14
Barley Mead DE14: Bur T 4H 13
   (off Grants Yd.)
Barn Cl. DE65: Fin 3K 7
Barns Ct. DE12: Cot E 6H 27
Barons Ct. DE14: Bur T 3G 13
Barr Cres. LE67: Whit 5G 35
Barrington Cl. DE13: Stre 5H 9
Barrys Cl. DE11: Wood 7B 22
Barton Bus. Pk. DE13: Bar N 1K 25
BARTON GATE 5D 16
Barton Ga. DE13: Bar N 5D 16
BARTON GREEN 7F 17
Barton Lodge DE13: Bar N 6H 17
Barton St. DE14: Bur T 7H 13
BARTON TURN 7K 17
Barton Turn DE13: Bar N 7J 17
Barton Turns DE13: Bar N 7K 17
BARTON-UNDER-NEEDWOOD 6G 17
Baslow Grn. DE11: New 3F 21
Bass Cotts. DE14: Bur T 3K 13
Bass's Cotts. DE14: Bur T 4G 13
Bass's Cres. DE11: Cas G 2F 29
Bath La. DE12: Moi 5K 29
Bath St. LE65: Ash Z 3A 32
Bath Yd. DE12: Moi 5A 30
Battleflat Dr. LE67: Ell 7F 41
Battleflat La. LE67: Ell 7J 41
Battlestead Hill 6A 12
Beacon Cres. LE67: Coal 2J 41
Beacon Dr. DE13: Rol D 3G 9
Beacon Rd. DE13: Rol D 4G 9
Beaconsfield Rd. DE13: Bur T 7F 9
Beadmans Cnr. LE67: Rav 1A 40
Beam Cl. DE13: Bur T 2E 6
BEAM HILL 6G 9
Beamhill Rd. DE13: Ans, Bur T 6D 8
Beards Rd. DE11: New 2H 21
Bearwood Hill Rd. DE15: Win 4A 14
Beatrice Ct. DE14: Bur T 3G 13
   (off Rangemore St.)
Beaufort Ct. DE15: Stap 6C 14
   (off Best Av.)
Beaufort Rd. DE15: Stap 6B 14
Beaumont Av. LE65: Ash Z 3J 31
Beaumont Grn. LE67: Cole 1K 33
Beaumont Rd. LE67: Whit 5H 35
Becket Cl. DE13: Bur T 1G 13
Becketts Ct. DE13: Bur T 7H 9
Bedale Cl. LE67: Coal 2D 40
Bedford Rd. DE15: Stap 1J 19
Beech Av. DE13: Stre 6A 10
   DE65: W'ton 1H 11
   LE67: Rav .2K 39
Beech Dr. DE11: Wood 6E 22
   DE13: Stre 6K 9
   DE65: Etw .1D 6
Beech Gro. DE11: New 1G 21
Beech La. DE13: Stre 5K 9
   (not continuous)
Beech Rd. DE13: Bar N 1G 25
Beech St. DE14: Bur T 6G 13
Beech Tree Rd. LE67: Coal 2H 41
Beech Way LE65: Ash Z 3C 32
   LE67: Ibs .6A 40
Beehive Av. DE12: Moi 5D 30
Beehive Farm Woodland Lake 4K 27
Beehives, The DE11: New 1H 21
Belcher Cl. LE67: Hea 7G 39
Belfield Ct. DE65: Etw 2C 6
Belfield Rd. DE11: Swad 4J 21
   DE65: Etw .2C 6
Belfield Ter. DE65: Etw 2C 6
Belfry, The DE13: Stre 5H 9
Belgrave Cl. LE67: Coal 1K 41
Bell La. DE11: Hart 5D 22
   DE13: Bar N 6G 17
Bells End Rd. DE12: Wal T 7C 18
Bellway Cl. LE67: Coal 7C 34
Belmont Dr. LE67: Coal 7B 34
Belmont St. DE11: Swad 4K 21
Belmot Rd. DE13: Tut 3A 8
Belton Cl. LE67: Coal 1K 41
Belvedere Rd. DE11: Wood 6C 22
   DE13: Bur T 1F 13
Belvoir Cl. DE13: Bur T 2G 13
Belvoir Cres. DE11: New 2H 21
Belvoir Dr. LE65: Ash Z 4A 32
Belvoir Rd. DE13: Bur T 2F 13
   LE67: Coal 1D 40
Belvoir Shop. Centre, The LE67: Coal 1D 40
Bend Oak Dr. DE15: Win 3D 14
Benenden Way LE65: Ash Z 2K 31
Bent La. DE65: Fos 1B 4

Bentley Brook DE65: Hilt 4K 5
Bentley Brook La. DE11: Hart 5D 22
Beowulf Covert DE13: Stre 5G 9
Beresford Dale DE11: Chu G 6G 21
Bernard Cl. LE67: Ibs 7B 40
Bernard Ct. DE11: Wood 5A 22
Bernard St. DE11: Wood 5A 22
Berrisford St. LE67: Coal 2D 40
Berry Cl. LE67: Rav 7B 34
Berry Gdns. DE15: Win 3D 14
Berry Hedge La. DE15: Win 3D 14
Berry Hill La. LE67: Don H 4C 40
Berwick Rd. LE65: Ash Z 4C 32
Best Av. DE15: Stap 6C 14
Betony Rd. DE15: Stap 5D 14
Beveridge La. LE67: Bar H, Ell 7F 41
Beverley Dr. DE14: Bran 1E 18
Bexley Dr. DE11: Chu G 7F 21
Birch Av. DE11: New 1G 21
    LE67: Whit 5H 35
Birch Cl. DE14: Bran 7F 13
Birches Cl. DE13: Stre 6J 9
Birchfield Rd. DE15: Stap 2K 19
Birch Gro. DE65: Hatt 3C 4
Birch Rd. LE65: Ash Z 2C 32
Birchwood Cl. LE67: Cole 6J 33
Birkdale Av. DE14: Bran 2F 19
Bishop Dale LE67: Thri 2E 34
Bishops Ga. DE11: Wood 6B 22
Bitham Ct. DE13: Stre 5H 9
Bitham La. DE13: Stre 5H 9
Blackbrook Ct. LE67: Coal 2J 41
Blackbrook Dr. LE67: Coal 2J 41
Black Eagle Ct. DE14: Bur T 3H 13
Blackett Dr. LE67: Hea 7G 39
BLACKFORDBY 1E 30
Blackfordby La. DE12: Moi 2E 30
Blackpool St. DE14: Bur T 7H 13
    ksmiths La. DE11: Wood 5C 22
    . New S 6F 11
    Egg 7B 6
Blacksmiths Yd. DE13: Rol D 2G 9
Blackthorn Rd. DE15: Stap 2K 19
Blackthorn Way DE12: Mea 4F 37
Blackwood LE67: Coal 1J 41
Bladon Ho's. DE15: New S 1C 14
Bladon St. DE15: Win 3D 14
Bladon's Yd. DE13: Rol D 2G 9
Bladon Vw. DE13: Stre 4A 10
Blakeholme Ct. DE14: Bur T 2H 13
Blakelow Dr. DE65: Etw 2C 6
Bleach Mill DE12: Mea 7F 37
Blenheim Cl. DE11: New 1H 21
    DE15: Win 4D 14
Blenheim M. DE65: Etw 1D 6
Blithe Cl. DE65: Hilt 4K 5
Bloom Cl. LE67: Rav 7B 34
Bloomfield Cl. DE65: Hilt 4J 5
Blossom Ri. DE11: New 2F 21
Blossom Wlk. DE65: Hatt 4B 4
Bluebell Cl. DE12: Don 1B 36
Blueberry Way DE11: Wood 5C 22
Blue Cedars Dr. DE15: Bret 5E 14
Blue Stone La. DE15: Stan 1A 20
Blythfield DE14: Bur T 3K 13
Boardman Ind. Est. DE11: Swad 5F 21
Boardman Rd. DE11: Swad 5F 21
Bob Southern Gro. DE11: Chu G 7J 21
Bodicote Way DE11: Swad 4A 22
Bodkin Row DE12: Oak 4E 36
Boothorpe La. LE67: Thri 1D 30
Booth Rd. LE67: Thri 1E 34
Borough Rd. DE14: Bur T 4H 13
Bosworth Cl. LE65: Ash Z 2B 32
Bosworth Dr. DE13: Bur T 1G 13
Bosworth Rd. DE12: Mea, Snar 5F 37
BOTANY BAY 6A 28
Botts Way LE67: Coal 3G 41
BOUNDARY 6F 23
Boundary Cl. DE13: Bur T 6G 9
Boundary Rd. DE65: Egg 5D 6
Bourne Cl. DE13: Tut 7A 4
Bourne Way DE11: Swad 4A 22
Bowens Cl. DE11: Wood 5C 22
Bowker Cres. LE65: Ash Z 4J 31
Box Cl. DE11: Wood 5B 22
Boylan Rd. LE67: Coal 7C 34
Bracken Cl. LE67: Hug 4D 40
Brackenwood Gro. DE15: Stap 2K 19

Bradfords La. LE67: Cole 2K 33
Bradgate Dr. DE11: Swad 2K 41
Bradley St. DE15: Stap 1K 19
Bradmore Rd. DE13: Bur T 2G 13
Bradshaw Mdw. DE65: Hatt 4B 4
Brailsford Av. DE11: New 3E 20
Bramble Ct. DE15: Stap 2K 19
Brambles Rd. LE67: Hug 4D 40
Bramble Wlk. DE12: Ove 6H 29
Bramblewood DE11: New 2G 21
Bramley Cl. DE14: Bran 1E 18
Bramley Ct. DE12: Moi 5D 30
Bramley Cl. DE65: Hatt 4B 4
Bramley Dale DE11: Chu G 6G 21
Bramling Cross Rd. DE14: Bur T 1A 14
BRANSTON 1D 18
Branston Golf Course 2G 19
Branston Rd. DE13: Stre 7A 12
    DE14: Bran, Tate 7B 12
    DE14: Bur T .7H 13
Branston Water Pk. 2B 18
Branston Water Pk. Vis. Cen. 1C 18
BREACH HILL 6E 32
Breach La. DE65: Fos 2B 4
Breach Rd. LE67: Coal 3E 40
Breadsall Cl. DE11: New 1H 21
Brendon Way LE65: Ash Z 4A 32
Bren Way DE65: Hilt 3K 5
BRETBY 4J 15
Bretby Bus. Pk. DE15: Bret 7G 15
Bretby Crematorium DE15: Bret 5G 15
Bretby Fairways DE15: Bret 5G 15
Bretby Hall DE15: Bret 5K 15
Bretby Hgts. DE11: Bret, New 1H 21
Bretby Hollow DE11: New 1G 21
Bretby La. DE15: Bret 5E 14
Bretby M. DE15: Bret 5J 15
Bretby Park 6J 15
Bretby Rd. DE11: New 2G 21
Bretby Stoneware Ind. Est. DE11: Bret . .7F 15
Bretby Vw. DE11: Hart 4D 22
Bretlands Way DE15: Stan 2B 20
Brewhouse Arts Cen. 5J 13
Briar Cl. DE11: Blac 1E 30
    DE11: New .2K 21
    LE67: Hug 3D 40
Brick Kiln Cft. DE12: Mea 4G 37
Brick Kiln La. DE13: Bar N 4D 16
    LE67: Ibs 7B 40
Bridge Cl. DE11: Chu G 6K 21
Bridge Farm M. DE13: Stre 5K 9
Bridge M. LE67: Whit 6E 34
Bridge Pl. LE65: Ash Z 2A 32
Bridge Rd. LE67: Coal 2E 40
Bridgeside DE13: Stre 5K 9
Bridge St. DE11: Cas G 1F 29
    DE11: Chu G 6K 21
    DE13: Stre 5K 9
    DE13: Tut 6B 4
    DE14: Bur T .4K 13
    DE65: Tut 6B 4
    LE65: Pac 1B 38
Bridgford Av. DE14: Bran 1E 18
Bridle La. DE15: Stan 4B 20
Bridle Rd. LE67: Coal 6D 34
Bridle Way DE11: Blac 7D 22
Briers Way LE67: Whit 4F 35
Brightman Ho. DE11: Swad 3J 21
Brindley Rd. LE67: Coal 7B 34
Bristol Av. LE65: Ash Z 5K 31
Bristol Ct. DE11: Chu G 7G 21
Britannia Dr. DE13: Stre 6J 9
Briton Lodge Cl. DE12: Moi 5C 30
Brittany Av. LE65: Ash Z 2K 31
Brizlincote La. DE15: Bret 6E 14
Brizlincote St. DE15: Stap 6A 14
Broadlands DE13: Stre 6J 9
Broad St. LE67: Coal 2E 40
Broadway St. DE14: Bur T 7H 13
Broadway Vs. DE11: New 2H 21
Bronte Cl. DE14: Bur T 7J 9
Brook Cl. DE65: Hatt 3C 4
    LE65: Pac 1A 38
Brookdale Rd. DE11: Hart 4D 22
Brook End DE65: Rep 3K 11
Brooker Cl. LE67: Coal 3K 11
Brook Ho. DE65: Rep 7K 11
Brook Ho. M. DE11: New 1H 21
    DE65: Rep 7K 11
Brook La. DE65: Fos 2B 4
    LE67: Thri 2E 34
Brooks Cl. DE12: Don 1C 36
Brookside DE13: Rol D 2G 9
    DE15: Win 2C 14
    LE65: Ash Z .3A 32
                   (off Brook St.)
Brook Side Cl. DE65: Rep 7K 11
Brookside Cres. LE67: Ibs 6B 40
Brookside Rd. DE13: Bar N 7F 17

Brooks La. LE67: Whit 4E 34
Brook St. DE11: Hart 1D 22
    DE11: New .2F 21
    DE11: Swad .5H 21
    DE14: Bur T .3J 13
    LE65: Ash Z .3A 32
Broomhalls Cft. DE13: Alre 7C 24
Broomhills La. DE65: Rep 7K 11
Broom Leys Av. LE67: Coal 2G 41
Broom Leys Rd. LE67: Coal 2F 41
Brouder Cl. LE67: Coal 2H 41
Brough Rd. DE15: Win 4D 14
Broughton Heath Golf Course 1C 4
Broughton Heath La. DE65: Fos, Hilt 1B 4
Broughton St. LE67: Coal 2E 40
Brown Ct. LE65: Ash Z 2J 31
Browning Dr. DE12: Mea 7E 36
Browning Rd. DE11: Swad 3K 21
Brown's La. DE13: Yox 2B 16
Brunel Dr. DE13: Stre 6A 10
Brunel Way DE11: Chu G 7F 21
    LE67: Coal 6C 34
Brunt La. DE11: Wood 5C 22
Brunt's La. DE65: Egg 7D 6
Bryan's Cl. LE67: Whit 3G 35
Bryony DE14: Bran 7G 13
Buckingham Cl. DE13: Stre 6J 9
Buckingham Cl. DE15: Win 4D 14
Buckingham Dr. DE11: Chu G 1G 29
Buckingham Ho. DE65: Hilt 4J 5
Buckingham Rd. LE67: Coal 1G 41
Buckley Cl. DE11: Wood 6C 22
    DE12: Mea 6F 37
Burdett Way DE65: Rep 7K 11
Burgess Rd. LE67: Coal 2D 40
BURNASTON 1G 7
Burnaston La. DE65: Etw 1D 6
Burns Cl. DE12: Mea 7E 36
Burnside DE13: Rol D 3G 9
Burnside Cl. DE13: Rol D 2G 9
                (off Bladon's Yd.)
BURNTHEATH 1H 5
Burrows, The DE11: New 3G 21
Burton Albion FC .7K 9
Burton Ent. Pk. DE14: Bur T 1K 13
Burton-on-Trent Golf Course 6F 15
Burton-on-Trent Station (Rail) 4H 13
Burton Pl. DE14: Bur T 5K 13
Burton Rd. DE11: Cas G 6E 20
    DE11: Mid, Wood 7H 15
    DE12: Cot E .6J 27
    DE12: Mea 5D 36
    DE12: Ove 3G 29
    DE12: Ros 3H 27
    DE13: Alre 6E 24
    DE13: Tut 6C 4
    DE14: Bran .1F 19
    DE65: Burn, Egg, Fin 7F 7
                (not continuous)
    DE65: Rep 5H 11
    LE65: Ash Z .7H 23
Burtons La. DE65: Swan 4B 34
Burton St. DE13: Tut 7B 4
BURTON UPON TRENT 4H 13
Burway Mdw. DE13: Alre 7D 24
BUSHTON 4A 8
Bushton La. DE13: Ans, Tut 4A 8
Butler Ct. DE14: Bur T 4G 13
Buttercup Cl. DE12: Don 1B 36
Buttercup Cl. DE15: Stap 6B 14
Buttercup Cl. LE67: Coal 2H 41
Butt La. DE11: Blac, Wood 6D 22
                (not continuous)
Butts Cft. DE13: Alre 6C 24
Buxton Cl. DE11: New 1H 21
Buzzard Cl. DE12: Mea 6E 36
Byrkley Ct. DE14: Bur T 4H 13
                 (off Byrkley St.)
Byrkley St. DE14: Bur T 3G 13
Byron Av. DE15: Stap 1K 19
Byron Cres. DE12: Mea 7F 37
Byron Rd. DE11: Swad 2K 21
Byrton Dr. LE67: Ell 6D 40

C

Cademan St. LE67: Whit 4G 35
CADLEY HILL 6E 20
Cadley Hill Ind. Est. DE11: Swad 6E 20
Cadley Hill Rd. DE11: Swad 6E 20
Cadley Hill Rdbt. DE11: Cas G 6E 20
Cadley La. DE11: Cas G 7B 20
    DE12: Cald 7B 20
    DE15: Drak 7K 19
Caernarvon Cl. DE13: Stre 6J 9
Caernarvon Vs. DE11: Mid 2B 22
             (off Winchester Dr.)
Cairns Cl. DE15: Win 4D 14

Calais Rd. DE13: Bur T 1G 13
Calder Cl. DE65: Hilt 4J 5
CALDWELL **2K 27**
Caldwell Cl. DE13: Lin 3A 28
   DE15: Drak .4H 19
Calgary Cres. DE15: Win 4E 14
Callingwood La. DE13: Tate 5A 12
Callis, The LE65: Ash Z 2A 32
Callister Way DE14: Bur T 5E 12
Cambrian Way DE11: Swad 5H 21
   LE65: Ash Z .4A 32
Cambridge St. DE14: Bur T 6G 13
   LE67: Coal 1F 41
Camelford La. LE67: Hug 3D 40
Camelot Cl. DE13: Stre 4K 9
Cameron Cl. DE15: Stap 6C 14
Campion Rd. DE11: Wood 4B 22
Canal Bri. DE11: W'ton 7H 7
Canal St. DE12: Oak 3D 36
   DE14: Bur T .5H 13
Canner Cl. DE11: Wood 6D 22
Cannock Cl. LE67: Ell 6E 40
Canterbury Dr. LE65: Ash Z 2K 31
Canterbury Rd. DE15: Win 4D 14
Capstan Cl. DE11: Wood 7B 22
Captain's La. DE13: Bar N 7F 17
Caraway Dr. DE14: Bran 7F 13
Carisbrooke Dr. DE13: Stre 5K 9
Carling Cl. LE67: Coal 1F 41
Carl Mt. Ho. DE11: Chu G 6H 21
Carlton Cl. DE14: Bur T 4G 13
             (off Shobnall Rd.)
Carlton St. DE13: Bur T 1G 13
Carnarvon Ct. DE15: Bret 5K 15
Caroline Cl. DE14: Bur T 5H 13
Carousels, The DE14: Bur T 2H 13
Carpenter Cl. DE15: Stap 5D 14
Carr Hill Rd. LE67: Whit 2F 35
Carriers Rd. DE65: Egg 6D 6
Carter Dale LE67: Whit 3E 34
Cartwright Ct. LE67: Bar H 5K 41
Cartwright Way LE67: Bar H 6K 41
Carver Rd. DE13: Bur T 1G 13
Casey La. DE14: Bur T 3G 13
Castilla Pl. DE13: Bur T 1H 13
Castle Ct. DE13: Tut 6B 4
Castle Cft. DE11: Cas G 1F 29
Castlegate DE13: Tut 6B 4
Castle Gate Ho. LE65: Ash Z 3A 32
CASTLE GRESLEY **7E 20**
Castle Hayes La. DE13: Tut 1A 8
Castle Hill DE65: Fin 3K 7
   LE67: Whit 4G 35
Castle Mews, The DE11: New 1H 21
Castle Pk. Rd. DE13: Bur T 7G 9
Castle Rd. DE11: Cas G 1F 29
Castle Rock Dr. LE67: Coal 7J 35
Castle St. DE13: Tut 6A 4
   LE67: Whit 4G 35
Castle Vw. DE65: Hatt 5B 4
Castle Way DE65: W'ton 7F 7
   LE65: Ash Z .5K 31
Catharine Ri. DE11: Chu G 7H 21
             (off Oxford St.)
CATHOLME **3H 25**
Catholme La. DE13: Bar N 3H 25
CATTON **6A 26**
Catton Hall **6A 26**
Catton La. DE12: Ros 5F 27
Catton Rd. DE12: Wal T 4A 26
Cavendish Cl. DE11: New 1H 21
Cavendish Cres. LE67: Hug 3D 40
Caxton Ct. DE14: Bur T 6J 13
Cecil Rd. DE11: New 3G 21
Cedar Cl. LE65: Ash Z 3C 32
Cedar Ct. LE67: Bar H 5K 41
Cedar Dr. LE67: Ibs 6A 40
Cedar Gro. DE11: New 1H 21
   DE12: Lin 3D 28
   DE12: Moi 3E 30
Cedar Rd. DE11: Cas G 2F 29
   DE13: Bar N .7G 17
Celandine Cl. DE15: Stap 5D 14
Celandine Pl. DE11: Wood 4B 22
Cello Cl. LE67: Whit 4F 35
Central Av. LE67: Ibs 7B 40
Central Cl. LE67: Coal 2E 40
Central Pas. LE67: Ibs 7B 40
Central Rd. LE67: Hug 3E 40
Central Way DE13: Bur T 7G 9
Centrum E. Retail Pk. DE14: Bur T 7D 12
Centrum One Hundred DE14: Bur T 6E 12
Century Theatre, The **1C 40**
Chandlers Cft. LE67: Ibs 5B 40
Channing Way LE67: Ell 6D 40
Chapel Cl. DE11: Alb V 7K 21
   DE65: W'ton .7J 7
   LE67: Rav 1A 40
Chapel Cft. DE12: Ros 3J 27

Chapel La. DE13: Ans 2A 12
   DE13: Rol D 2G 9
   LE67: Cole 1K 33
Chapel St. DE11: Cas G 1F 29
   DE11: Chu G .7H 21
   DE11: New 2G 21
   DE11: Wood .6B 22
   DE12: Cot E .6J 27
   DE12: Don 1B 36
   DE12: Mea 5F 37
   DE12: Oak 4C 36
   LE65: Smis 5J 23
   LE67: Ibs 6B 40
Chapmans Cft. DE12: Cot E 6J 27
Chapmans Mdws. LE65: Ash Z 5B 32
Charles St. DE11: Chu G 6J 21
   LE67: Coal 7B 34
Charleston Ct. DE11: New 1H 21
Charlotte Ct. DE11: Swad 3K 21
   DE14: Bur T .7H 13
Charlton Cl. DE12: Lin 4D 28
Charnborough Ct. LE67: Coal 2J 41
Charnborough Rd. LE67: Coal 1J 41
Charnwood Rd. DE13: Bur T 7G 9
Charnwood St. LE67: Coal 2F 41
Charter Point Way LE65: Ash Z 3D 32
Chase, The DE12: Ros 3H 27
Chaseview Rd. DE13: Alre 7C 24
Chatfield Cl. DE15: Stap 6D 14
Chatsworth Dr. DE13: Tut 7B 4
Chatsworth Rd. DE11: New 2H 21
Chattens Mdw. DE11: Cas G 1G 29
Chaucer Cl. DE14: Bur T 1J 13
Cheedale Cl. DE15: Win 2B 14
Chelmsford Cl. DE11: Chu G 7F 21
Cheltenham Dr. LE65: Ash Z 2K 31
Cherry Cl. DE14: Bran 7F 13
Cherry Gth. DE65: Hilt 3J 5
Cherry Leys DE15: Win 3D 14
Cherry Tree Cl. DE11: New 2G 21
   DE65: Hilt 3J 5
Cherry Tree Ct. DE12: Moi 3E 30
Cherry Tree Gdns. DE15: Win 4D 14
Cherry Tree M. DE11: Wood 6C 22
Cherry Tree Rd. DE15: Stap 2A 20
Chesterfield Av. DE11: New 2F 21
Chesterfield Dr. DE12: Lin 3D 28
Chester Gdns. DE11: Chu G 6J 21
Chesterton Rd. DE14: Bur T 7J 9
Chestnut Av. DE11: Mid 2J 21
Chestnut Cl. DE12: Moi 4E 30
   LE67: Ibs 7A 40
Chestnut Dr. DE13: Bur T 7G 9
Chestnut Grn. DE11: Chu G 6J 21
Chestnut Gro. DE65: Etw 1C 6
   LE67: Coal 2J 41
Chestnut M. DE15: Stap 2A 20
Chestnut Rd. DE15: Stap 1A 20
Chestnut Way DE65: Rep 4K 11
Chevin, The DE13: Stre 5H 9
Cheviot Cl. DE11: Swad 5H 21
Chichester Cl. LE67: Ell 6D 40
Chilcott Cl. LE67: Coal 1G 41
Chiltern Ri. LE65: Ash Z 4B 32
Chiltern Rd. DE11: Swad 5G 21
Chilton Cl. DE13: Stre 5K 9
             (off Bridge St.)
Chiswell Dr. LE67: Coal 7C 34
Christ Church M. LE67: Coal 1E 40
Christopher Cl. LE67: Ibs 5B 40
Chrysanthemum Ct. DE11: New 3H 21
Church Av. DE11: Swad 5J 21
   DE65: Hatt 5C 4
Church Broughton Rd. DE65: Fos 3B 4
Church Cl. DE11: Blac 7E 22
   DE15: Win 3C 14
   DE65: W'ton .1J 11
Church Cft. DE12: Cot E 6H 27
Churchfields DE13: Yox 2B 16
CHURCH GRESLEY **6J 21**
Church Gresley Indoor Bowls Cen. **6G 21**
Church Gresley Ind. Est.
   DE11: Chu G .1H 29
Church Hill DE65: Etw 1C 6
   LE67: Swan .2C 34
Church Hill St. DE15: Win 4C 14
Churchill Cl. LE65: Ash Z 3J 31
Churchill Cres. DE13: Alre 7C 24
Churchill Dr. DE65: Hilt 3K 5
Church La. DE12: Cald 2K 27
   DE13: Bar N .7G 17
   DE15: New S 6E 10
   LE67: Rav 6K 39
   LE67: Swan, Whit 4C 34
Church M. DE65: Hatt 4C 4
Church Rd. DE11: New 2H 21
   DE13: Alre 6C 24
   DE13: Rol D, Tut 1D 8
   DE13: Stre 5K 9

Church Rd. DE14: Bran 1D 18
   DE65: Egg 1C 10
Churchside DE65: W'ton 1H 11
Churchside Wlk. LE65: Ash Z 3A 32
          (off Kilwardby St.)
Church St. DE11: Chu G 7H 21
   DE11: Hart 2E 22
   DE11: New 2H 21
   DE11: Swad .4K 21
   DE12: Cot E .6H 27
   DE12: Don 2B 36
   DE13: Tut 6B 4
CHURCH TOWN **3H 33**
Church Vw. DE13: Bur T 7H 9
   DE13: Rol D 2F 9
   LE67: Ibs 7A 40
Church Wlk. DE12: Don 2B 36
           (off Church St.)
Churchward Dr. DE13: Stre 5A 10
Church Way DE12: Ove 7J 29
Church Yd. LE65: Ash Z 3B 32
Churnet Ct. DE14: Bur T 3K 13
Churnet Rd. DE65: Hilt 5J 5
Cineworld Cinema
   Burton upon Trent **4J 13**
City, The DE11: Wood 6C 22
             (not continuous)
City of Dan LE67: Whit 5G 35
City of Three Waters LE67: Whit 3F 35
Civic Way DE11: Swad 4J 21
Clamp Dr. DE11: Swad 5J 21
Claremont Dr. LE67: Coal, Rav 7A 34
Clarence Dr. LE67: Coal 2G 41
Clarence Pl. LE65: Ash Z 3C 32
Clarence St. DE14: Bur T 6H 13
Claridge Pl. LE65: Ash Z 3A 32
Clarke Cl. LE67: Whit 5G 35
Clarke Ind. Est. DE14: Bur T 4K 13
Clarke Rd. LE67: Coal 2K 41
Claverhouse Rd. DE15: Bur T 5B 14
Clay Cl. DE11: Swad 4A 22
Clay La. LE67: Cole 1B 34
   LE67: Ell 7F 41
Claymar Dr. DE11: New 1H 21
CLAY MILLS **4A 10**
Claymills Pumping Station **6B 10**
Claymills Rd. DE13: Stre 4A 10
Clays Ct. DE14: Bran 1E 18
Clay's La. DE14: Bran 7E 12
Clay St. DE15: Stap 6A 14
Clay St. E. DE15: Stap 6B 14
Cleave Rd. DE14: Bran 7F 13
Clematis Cres. DE15: Stap 7B 14
Cleveland Cl. DE11: Swad 5J 21
Clewley Rd. DE14: Bran 7E 12
Cliffe Hill Rail Terminal LE67: Bar H 6H 41
Clifton Av. LE65: Ash Z 1A 32
Clifton Cl. DE11: Swad 6H 21
   DE12: Ove 6H 29
Clifton Dr. LE65: Ash Z 2K 31
Cliftonthorpe Mdws. LE65: Ash Z 7K 23
Clifton Way DE15: Stap 5C 14
Clink La. LE67: Swan 5B 34
Clive Ho. DE15: Win 4D 14
Cloisters, The DE15: Stap 6A 14
Close, The DE11: Alb V 1A 30
   DE12: Lin 4D 28
   DE13: Tut 7A 4
   DE15: New S 1C 14
Close Bank DE13: Tut 7B 4
Close Banks Wlk. DE13: Tut 7B 4
Clough Dr. DE14: Bur T 1K 13
Clover Ct. DE14: Bran 2D 18
Cloverdale DE11: Mid 1J 21
Clover Pl. LE67: Thri 1E 34
Cloverslade DE65: Fin 4K 7
Clutsom Rd. LE67: Coal 3D 40
Clyde Ct. LE67: Thri 1E 34
Clyde St. DE65: Hilt .4J 5
Coach Ho. M. DE11: New 1H 21
Coach Way DE65: W'ton 1J 11
Coalfield Way LE65: Ash Z 3C 32
Coal Pit La. DE12: Cot E 6J 27
COALVILLE **1D 40**
Coalville Bus. Cen. LE67: Coal 7E 34
Coalville Bus. Pk. LE67: Coal 1D 40
COALVILLE COMMUNITY HOSPITAL **1H 41**
Coalville La. LE67: Coal, Rav 1A 40
COLEORTON **2K 33**
Coleorton Hall LE67: Cole 2H 33
Coleorton La. LE65: Pac 7B 32
COLEORTON MOOR **3K 33**
Coleridge Cl. DE14: Bur T 1J 13
         (off Horninglow Rd.)
College Cl. LE67: Coal 2D 40
Colliers Cl. DE11: New 2F 21
Colliers Way LE67: Ell 7F 41
Colliery La. DE12: Lin 5E 28
Colliery Railway **1B 40**

Colliery Rd. DE11: Chu G 1H 29
Colliery Row DE11: Chu G ...7H 21
Collinson Rd. DE13: Bar N ...7G 17
Colonel Cl. LE67: Ell 7E 40
Coltsfoot Cl. DE11: Wood ...4C 22
Comet Way LE67: Coal 7D 34
Common End DE65: Etw 6A 12
Common La. DE13: Tate 6A 12
Common Rd. DE11: Chu G ...7J 21
Common Side DE11: Chu G ...6K 21
Conifers, The DE12: Ove ...3H 29
Coniston Cl. DE11: Swad ...4J 21
   (off Darklands Rd.)
Coniston Gdns. LE65: Ash Z ...4B 32
Conkers **4B 30**
Conkers Waterside **5A 30**
Constable Way LE67: Cole ...2H 33
Convent Cl. DE15: Stap ...7A 14
Convent Dr. LE67: Coal ...2E 40
Conway Cl. DE13: Stre 6J 9
Cooper Cl. LE67: Whit 4E 34
Coopers Cft. DE65: Hatt ...4B 4
Cooper's Lodge DE14: Bur T ...4H 13
   (off Grants Yd.)
Cooper's Sq. DE14: Bur T ...5J 13
Cophills Cl. DE12: Mea ...6F 37
Copperas Rd. DE11: New ...3E 20
Coppice Cl. LE67: Rav 7A 34
Coppice Side DE11: Swad ...6K 21
Copse Cl. LE67: Hug 3D 40
Copse Ri. DE11: Mid 1J 21
Copson St. LE67: Ibs 7B 40
Corden Av. DE13: Stre 6A 10
Corkscrew La. LE65: Pac ...5D 32
   LE67: Cole 4E 32
Cornfield Cl. LE67: Ell 7F 41
Cornmill Balk DE13: Tut ...7C 4
Cornmill La. DE13: Tut 7B 4
Cornwall Rd. DE15: Stap ...2K 19
Coronation Av. DE12: Moi ...3E 30
Coronation La. DE12: Oak ...4C 36
Coronation St. DE11: Swad ...3H 21
   DE12: Ove 5H 29
Costello Cl. LE67: Ibs 5B 40
COTON IN THE ELMS **6H 27**
Coton La. DE12: Ros 5J 27
COTON PARK **1D 28**
Coton Pk. DE12: Lin 6C 20
Coton Rd. DE12: Wal T 7C 18
Cotswold Cl. DE11: Swad ...5H 21
Cotswold Rd. DE14: Bran ...7E 12
Cotswold Way LE65: Ash Z ...4B 32
Cottage Cl. DE11: New 2H 21
Cottesmore Cl. DE15: Stap ...6B 14
Cotton Cl. DE13: Alre 6C 24
Court Farm La. DE14: Bran ...1D 18
Courtland Rd. DE65: Etw ...2C 6
Courtney Cl. LE67: Whit ...6F 35
Court St. DE11: Wood 5B 22
Courtyard, The LE67: Coal ...7E 34
Coventry Cl. DE11: Mid ...2A 22
Coverdale LE67: Whit 3F 35
Covert Pl. DE11: Alb V 1K 29
Cowslip Cl. DE12: Don 7H 9
Crackpotz **6D 24**
Crafty Flats La.
   DE12: Cot E 7K 27
Cragdale LE67: Whit 2E 34
Cranfield Av. DE11: Chu G ...6F 21
Craven St. DE13: Bur T 1H 13
CRAYTHORNE **4J 9**
Craythorne Cl. DE11: New ...1H 21
Craythorne Golf Course **3H 9**
Craythorne Rd. DE13: Stre ...3G 9
Crescent, The DE11: New ...2F 21
   DE65: Rep 7K 11
Crescent Rd. LE67: Hug ...3D 40
Crest, The DE12: Lin 4D 28
Crest Cl. DE13: Stre 5K 9
Crestwood Cl. DE13: Stre ...6J 9
Creswell Dr. LE67: Rav 2K 39
Crichton Av. DE13: Stre 7J 9
Crich Way DE11: New 3F 21
Cricket Cl. DE15: New S ...6F 11
Cricketers, The DE13: Alre ...7C 24
Cricketers Cl. DE15: Stap ...7A 14
Croft, The DE11: New 2F 21
   DE12: Mea 5E 36
   DE15: Stap 6A 14
   LE65: Ash Z 4C 32
   LE67: Rav 2A 40
Croft Cl. DE13: Rol D 2G 9
Cromore Cl. LE67: Coal ...1K 41
Cromwell Cl. DE13: Tut ...1B 8
   LE65: Ash Z 2C 32
Cropston Dr. LE67: Coal ...2H 41
Cross, The DE65: Rep 3K 11
Cross La. DE13: Rol D 4G 9
Crossman St. DE14: Bur T ...4F 13

Cross St. DE11: Cas G 1F 29
   DE14: Bur T 5H 13
Cross St. Bus. Cen. DE14: Bur T ...4H 13
Crowberry La. DE13: Bar N ...6G 17
Crown Ind. Est. DE14: Bur T ...5G 13
Crown Ri. DE11: Wood 5A 22
Crown Sq. DE14: Bur T 7D 12
Croxall Rd. DE13: Alre 7F 24
Crusader Cl. LE67: Whit ...4G 35
Culland Rd. DE14: Bran ...6E 40
Cumberland Rd. DE15: Stap ...1J 19
   LE67: Ell 6E 40
Curlew Cl. LE67: Coal 2H 41
Curtis Ct. DE13: Bur T 7H 9
Curtis Way DE14: Bur T 3G 13
Curzon St. DE14: Bur T 4G 13
   LE67: Ibs 7B 40
Curzon St. W. DE14: Bur T ...4G 13
Cutting, The DE11: Hart ...4C 22
Cyclamen Cl. DE14: Bran ...7F 13

D

Daisy Cl. DE12: Don 1B 36
   LE67: Coal 2H 41
Daisy La. DE12: Ove 6J 29
   DE13: Alre 7A 24
   (not continuous)
Dale Brook DE65: Hilt 4K 5
Dalebrook Rd. DE15: Win ...2B 14
Dale End La. DE65: Hilt 2H 5
Dale End Rd. DE65: Hilt ...3H 5
Dalefield Dr. DE11: Swad ...5J 21
Dale Gdns. DE12: Mea 5G 37
Dales Cl. DE11: New 3F 21
Daleside DE15: Stap 6C 14
Dale St. DE14: Bur T 5H 13
Dalkeith Wlk. LE67: Thri ...1E 34
Dallow Cl. DE14: Bur T 2H 13
Dallow Cres. DE14: Bur T ...2H 13
Dallow St. DE14: Bur T 2G 13
Dalston Rd. DE11: New 3H 21
Dalton Av. DE15: Stap 5C 14
Dame Paulet Wlk. DE14: Bur T ...1H 13
Darklands La. DE11: Swad ...4H 21
Darklands Rd. DE11: Swad ...4J 21
Dark La. DE13: Alre 6D 24
   DE13: Tate 6A 12
Darley Cl. DE11: Cas G 7H 21
   DE15: Stap 6D 14
Darley Dale DE11: Chu G ...6G 21
Darwin Cl. DE11: Mid 6D 14
Dauphine Cl. LE67: Coal ...1K 41
   (off Romans Cres.)
Davenport Way DE11: Wood ...7C 22
David Lees Cl. LE67: Ell ...7F 41
Davis Rd. DE11: Swad 4J 21
Dawkins Rd. DE12: Don ...1B 36
Daybell Rd. DE12: Moi 5D 30
Dayton Cl. LE67: Coal 7B 34
Dee Cl. DE65: Hilt 4K 5
Deepdale Cl. DE15: Win ...2C 14
   LE67: Ibs 6B 40
Deepdene Cl. DE11: Chu G ...7K 21
Deepmore Cl. DE13: Alre ...7D 24
De Ferrers Cft. DE13: Stre ...6H 9
De Ferrers Pl. DE12: Lin ...4F 29
Degens Way LE67: Hug ...3C 40
Delhi Cl. DE15: Win 4H 13
De Montfort Cl. DE11: Chu G ...7F 21
Denbigh Cl. DE13: Stre 7J 9
Denby Turn DE14: Bur T ...2J 13
Dennis Barsby Cl. DE11: Swad ...5F 21
Dennis St. LE67: Hug 4E 40
Denstone Cl. LE65: Ash Z ...1K 31
Denton Ri. DE13: Bur T 7F 9
Denton Rd. DE13: Bur T 1F 13
Dents Rd. LE65: Ash Z 2C 32
Derby Rd. DE11: Hart 1H 23
   DE11: Swad 4K 21
   DE13: Bur T, Stre 1K 13
   DE14: Bur T 2J 13
   DE65: Etw, Hilt 3J 5
   DE65: Fos, Hilt 3C 4
   DE65: Stre 4B 10
   DE73: Tick 1H 23
   LE65: Ash Z 2A 32
   LE65: Smis 1H 23
Derby Southern By-Pass
   DE65: Burn, Etw, Fin, Hilt ...2A 6
Derby St. DE14: Bur T 4H 13
Derby St. E. DE14: Bur T ...3H 13
Derry's Hollow LE67: Ell ...7F 41
De Ruthyn Cl. DE12: Moi ...5D 30
Derwent Cl. DE11: Cas G ...7H 21
   DE14: Bur T 4K 13
Derwent Ct. DE65: W'ton ...7H 7
Derwent Gdns. LE65: Ash Z ...5B 32

Derwent Pk. DE14: Bur T 2J 13
Derwent Rd. DE15: Stap 6B 14
Devana Av. LE67: Coal 2G 41
Deveron Cl. DE13: Stre 5H 9
   LE67: Coal 1K 41
Devon Cl. DE12: Moi 3F 31
   DE15: Stap 2K 19
Dibble Rd. DE14: Bran 1F 19
Dickens Cl. DE14: Bur T ...1J 13
Dickens Dr. DE11: Swad ...3K 21
Dingle, The DE15: Stap ...7K 13
Dingle Dr. DE13: Bur T ...2D 12
Dinmore Grange DE11: Hart ...2E 22
Discovery Cl. LE67: Coal ...7C 34
Discovery Driving Range & Golf Cen. **1B 40**
Discovery Way LE65: Ash Z ...2C 32
Doctor's Walk, The DE12: Mea ...5F 37
Dodslow Av. DE13: Rol D 3G 9
Dogshead La. DE13: Bar N ...1F 25
Doles La. DE65: Fin 2K 7
Dominion Rd. DE11: Swad ...3J 21
Donington Dr. DE11: Wood ...7B 22
   LE65: Ash Z 4K 31
DONINGTON LE HEATH **4D 40**
Donington le Heath Manor House & Gardens
   ....**4D 40**
DONISTHORPE **1B 36**
Donisthorpe La. DE12: Moi ...6A 30
Donisthorpe Woodland Pk. ...**7C 30**
Donithorne Cl. DE13: Bur T ...7H 9
Dorset Cl. DE15: Stap 2K 19
Dorset Dr. DE12: Moi 3F 31
Douglas Dr. LE67: Ibs 7B 40
Dovecliff Cres. DE13: Stre ...4A 10
Dovecliff Rd. DE13: Rol D, Stre ...2K 9
Dove Cl. DE11: Wood 5C 22
Dovedale Cl. DE15: Win ...3B 14
Dove Gro. DE65: Egg 1B 10
Dovelea DE13: Rol D 2G 9
Dover Ct. DE13: Bur T 7H 9
Doveridge Rd. DE15: Stap ...5C 14
Dove Ri. DE65: Hilt 3H 5
Dove Rd. LE67: Coal 3H 41
Dover Rd. DE13: Bur T 7G 9
Dove Side DE65: Hatt 5C 4
Dove Valley Pk. DE65: Fos ...1A 4
Dove Vw. DE13: Tut 7B 4
Downside Dr. LE65: Ash Z ...2K 31
DRAKELOW **3J 19**
Drakelow Rd. DE12: Wal T ...7C 18
Dray Ct. DE14: Bur T 4H 13
   (Grants Yd.)
   DE14: Bur T 5H 13
   (Uxbridge St.)
Drayton St. DE11: Swad 4K 21
Drew Cl. LE65: Ash Z 2A 32
Drift Cl. DE11: Blac 1E 30
Driftside DE11: Blac 2E 30
Drive, The DE13: Bur T 7H 9
Drome Cl. LE67: Coal 1K 41
   (off Romans Cres.)
Dromintee Rd. LE67: Bar H ...6J 41
Dryden Cl. DE12: Mea 6F 37
Dryer Cl. LE67: Ibs 7B 40
Duchess Cl. DE12: Lin 4D 28
Duchy Cl. DE13: Stre 6K 9
Duck St. DE65: Egg 1B 10
Duke St. DE13: Tut 7B 4
   DE14: Bur T 5H 13
Dumps Rd. LE67: Whit 3F 35
Dunbar Rd. LE67: Coal 2K 41
Dunbar Way LE65: Ash Z ...4B 32
Dundee Rd. DE11: Mid 3A 22
Dunedin Cres. DE15: Win ...5D 14
Dunnsmoor La. DE11: Hart ...1A 22
Dunsmore Way DE11: Mid ...3A 22
DUNSTALL **3G 17**
Dunstall Brook DE15: Stap ...6B 14
Dunstall Cross DE13: Ran ...2D 16
Dunstall Hill DE13: Dun ...2E 16
Dunstall Rd. DE13: Bar N ...6G 17
   DE13: Tate 2J 17
Durban Cl. DE15: Win 4D 14
Durham Cl. DE11: Mid 3B 22
Durris Cl. LE67: Coal 1K 41
DW Fitness
   Burton upon Trent **4K 13**
Dyson's Cl. DE12: Mea 6E 36

E

Eagle Cl. DE12: Mea 6E 36
Eagle Hgts. DE15: Win 4E 14
Ealand St. DE13: Rol D 2H 9
Earls Ct. DE13: Stre 6J 9
East Cl. DE11: Chu G 7F 21
East Cres. LE67: Ell 7F 41
East End Dr. DE11: Swad ...4K 13

Eastern Av. DE13: Stre 6A 10
Eastfield Rd. DE11: Mid 2K 21
East Lawn DE65: Fin 3K 7
East St. DE15: Win 4C 14
East Wlk. LE67: Ibs 7B 40
Eaton Cl. DE65: Hatt 4C 4
Eccleshall Bus. Pk. DE14: Bur T 3K 13
Eden Cl. DE65: Hilt 5H 5
Edgecote Dr. DE11: New 1H 21
Edgehill Way LE65: Ash Z 2C 32
Edinburgh Rd. DE11: Chu G 7F 21
Edinburgh Way DE13: Stre 6J 9
Edmonton Pl. DE15: Win 4E 14
Edward St. DE11: Alb V 7K 21
  DE11: Hart 5D 22
  DE12: Ove .5H 29
  DE14: Bur T 3G 13
EFFLINCH **2H 25**
Efflinch La. DE13: Bar N 7G 17
EGGINTON **1C 10**
Egginton Rd. DE65: Egg, Hilt 3J 5
  DE65: Etw .4C 6
  (not continuous)
Eighth Av. DE14: Bur T 7E 12
Eldon St. DE15: Win 4C 14
Electric St. DE14: Bur T 2K 13
Electric St. Ind. Est. DE14: Bur T 2K 13
Elford St. LE65: Ash Z 3A 32
Elgin Wlk. LE67: Thri 1E 34
Elizabeth Av. DE13: Rol D 3G 9
  LE67: Ibs .6B 40
Elizabeth Ct. DE15: Win 4D 14
Ellis Cl. LE67: Ell 7F 41
ELLISTOWN **7E 40**
Elm Av. LE65: Ash Z 2C 32
Elm Cl. DE14: Bran 7E 12
  LE67: Ibs .6A 40
Elm Dr. DE65: Hilt 3J 5
Elm Gro. DE12: Moi 3E 30
Elmhurst DE65: Egg 1B 10
Elms, The LE67: Whit 4E 34
Elmsdale Rd. DE11: Hart 5D 22
Elms Gro. DE65: Etw 2D 6
Elmslea Av. DE12: Cot E 6J 27
Elmsleigh Cl. DE11: Mid 2J 21
Elmsleigh Dr. DE11: Mid 2J 21
Elmsleigh Grn. DE11: Mid 2J 21
Elms Rd. DE12: Cot E 6H 27
  DE15: Stap 5A 14
Elsdon Cl. LE67: Whit 4E 34
Elstead La. DE11: Blac 7E 22
Elton Way LE67: Ell 7F 41
Elvaston Cl. LE65: Ash Z 4B 32
Elwyn Cl. DE13: Stre 5J 9
Ely Cl. DE11: Mid 2A 22
Emery Cl. DE12: Lin 4E 28
Empire Rd. DE15: Win 4E 14
End, The DE15: New S 6F 11
Enderby Ri. DE13: Bur T 7F 9
Enfield Cl. DE65: Hilt 3K 5
Ennerdale Gdns. LE65: Ash Z 4C 32
Ensor Cl. DE11: Swad 3A 22
Epsom Cl. DE14: Bran 1E 18
Epworth Ho. DE15: Win 4E 14
Ernest Hall Way DE11: Swad 4K 21
Escolme Cl. DE11: Swad 4A 22
Essex Dr. DE11: Chu G 1F 29
Essex Rd. DE15: Stap 2J 19
Essington Cl. DE13: Alre 6D 24
Eton Bus. Pk. DE14: Bur T 1K 13
Eton Cl. DE14: Bur T 1K 13
  LE65: Ash Z 1K 31
Eton Pk. DE14: Bur T 1K 13
Eton Rd. DE14: Bur T 1J 13
Etta's Way DE65: Etw 1C 6
ETWALL **1C 6**
Etwall By-Pass DE65: Etw 1B 6
Etwall Leisure Cen. **1C 6**
Etwall Rd. DE65: Egg 5C 6
  DE65: W'ton 5H 7
Eureka Rd. DE11: Mid 3K 21
Eveden Cl. LE67: Whit 4F 35
Evergreens, The DE13: Stre 6A 10
Evershed Way DE14: Bur T 5H 13
EVISA Health & Fitness Club **5H 21**
Excelsior Dr. DE11: Wood 6B 22
Excelsior Rd. LE65: Ash Z 2D 32
Exchange Ct. DE15: Stap 1K 19
Exchange Rd. DE13: Alre 6D 24
Exeter Cl. DE11: Mid 2B 22
Exmoor Cl. LE67: Ell 6E 40
Eyam Cl. DE15: Stap 5C 14
Eyrie, The DE15: Win 4D 14

F

Fabis Cl. DE11: Swad 5H 21
Fairfax Cl. LE65: Ash Z 2C 32

Fairfield LE67: Ibs 7B 40
Fairfield Av. DE13: Rol D 2J 9
Fairfield Ct. LE67: Hug 4D 40
Fairfield Cres. DE11: New 3F 21
Fairfield Rd. LE67: Hug 4D 40
Fairfield Ter. DE11: Wood 5C 22
Fairham Rd. DE13: Stre 4A 10
Fairway DE14: Bran 2G 19
Fairway, The DE11: New 3F 21
Falaise Way DE65: Hilt 3K 5
Falcon Cl. DE14: Bur T 2K 13
Falcon Way DE11: Wood 5C 22
Faldo Cl. DE14: Bran 2G 19
Fallowfield Dr. DE13: Bar N 6F 17
Faraday Av. DE13: Stre 6J 9
Faraday Ct. DE14: Bur T 1D 18
Farm Cl. DE13: Bur T 7G 9
  DE65: Hilt .4H 5
Farm Ct. Flats DE13: Bur T 7H 9
  (off Farm Rd.)
Farm La. DE15: New S 7E 10
  LE67: Don H 4C 40
Farm Rd. DE13: Bur T 7H 9
Farm Side DE11: New 3G 21
FARM TOWN **3G 33**
Farm Town La. LE67: Cole 3G 33
Farndale LE67: Whit 3E 34
Fauld La. DE13: Tut 7A 4
Faversham Rd. DE13: Bur T 1F 13
Featherbed La. LE65: Ash Z 2C 32
Femwork Ind. Est. DE14: Bur T 2K 13
Fenelon Cl. DE11: Wood 7B 22
Fenton Av. DE11: Blac 7E 22
Fenton Cl. DE12: Mea 7E 36
Fenton Cres. DE12: Mea 7F 37
Fenton Grn. DE13: Stre 5K 9
Fern Av. DE65: W'ton 7K 7
Fern Cl. DE65: W'ton 7K 7
Ferndale LE67: Ibs 7A 40
Ferrers Av. DE13: Tut 1A 8
Ferrers Cl. LE65: Ash Z 4J 31
Ferrers Rd. DE13: Yox 2A 16
  LE67: Whit 5G 35
Ferry Grn. DE65: W'ton 1J 11
Ferry St. DE15: Stap 1K 19
Ferry Va. Cl. DE15: Stap 7K 13
Festival Rd. DE14: Bran 1D 18
Fettes Cl. LE65: Ash Z 1K 31
Fiddler's La. DE13: Tut 3D 8
Field Av. DE65: Hatt 4B 4
Field Cl. DE13: Bur T 7F 9
  DE65: Hilt .3J 5
  LE67: Thri .2E 34
Field Dr. DE13: Rol D 2G 9
Field Ho. DE65: Rep 4K 11
Field La. DE11: Bou 6F 23
  DE13: Bur T 7D 8
Field Ri. DE13: Bur T 7F 9
Fields La. DE11: Cas G 3G 29
Field Vw. DE11: Wood 3B 22
  LE67: Whit 4E 34
Field Way DE11: New 3G 21
  (off South Dr.)
Fifth Av. DE14: Bur T 5F 13
Finch Cl. DE11: Wood 5C 22
FINDERN **3K 7**
Findern La. DE65: Burn 1H 7
  DE65: W'ton 7H 7
Finings Ct. DE14: Bur T 5H 13
Finney Cl. DE12: Don 1B 36
First Av. DE14: Bur T 1D 18
Fir Tree Wlk. DE12: Moi 3E 30
  (off Ashfield Dr.)
Fisher Cl. DE65: Rep 7K 11
Fishpond La. DE13: Tut 7A 4
  DE65: Egg 1B 10
Flour Mills, The
  DE15: Bur T 2B 14
Fitness First
  Burton upon Trent **3K 13**
Fivelands Rd. DE15: Stap 7A 14
Flagstaff 42 Bus. Pk.
  LE65: Ash Z 1C 32
Flannagan Way LE67: Coal 3J 41
Flatts Cl. DE13: Bur T 1G 13
  LE67: Ibs .5B 40
Flax Cft. DE65: Hatt 4B 4
Fleet St. DE14: Bur T 5J 13
Fletches, The DE13: Stre 5G 9
Flora Gro. LE65: Ash Z 3B 32
Floret Cl. LE67: Rav 7B 34
Flour Mills, The
  DE15: Bur T 2B 14
Foan Hill LE67: Swan 5C 34
Fontwell Rd. DE14: Bran 1E 18
Fordice Cl. LE67: Hug 3D 40
Ford La. DE65: W'ton 1J 11
Ford St. DE15: Stap 1K 19
Forest Bus. Pk. LE67: Bar H 6K 41
Forest Edge Way DE13: Bur T 6F 9
Forest Lea DE12: Moi 5B 30

Forest Rd. DE11: Blac 7D 22
  DE13: Bar N, Dun 5D 16
  DE13: Bur T 2C 12
  LE67: Coal 3E 40
Forest School St. DE13: Rol D 2H 9
Forest Vw. DE12: Ove 5J 29
Forge Cl. DE65: Rep 7K 11
Forge La. DE13: Stre 4A 10
Forman Cl. DE11: Swad 4J 21
Formans Way LE67: Rav 7B 34
Forrester Cl. LE67: Cole 5J 33
Forties La. LE65: Smis 4J 23
Fosbrooke Cl. LE67: Rav 2K 39
Foss Rd. DE65: Hilt 4K 5
Foster Rd. DE11: Wood 6C 22
Foston Av. DE13: Bur T 1F 13
Foston Cl. DE65: Hilt 5B 4
Foston/Hatton/Hilton By-Pass DE65: Fos, Hilt . .1A 4
Fourth Av. DE14: Bur T 5E 12
Fox Cl. DE14: Bran 7G 13
Fox Fld. DE11: Cas G 1G 29
Foxglove Av. DE12: Don 1B 36
  DE15: Stap 7B 14
Foxglove Rd. LE67: Coal 2H 41
Fox La. DE13: Alre 7C 24
Foxton Cl. DE13: Alre 7D 24
Francis Way LE67: Ell 7F 41
Frank Bodicote Way DE11: Swad, Wood .5K 21
Franklin Cl. DE15: Stap 6C 14
Franks Rd. LE67: Bar H 6K 41
Frearson Rd. LE67: Hug 3C 40
Fred Brewer Way DE13: Bur T 3D 12
Frederick St. DE11: Wood 5B 22
  DE15: Stap 7K 13
Friars Wlk. DE14: Bur T 5K 13
Friary Cft. DE11: New 1H 21
Fullbrook Av. DE13: Bar N 1G 25
Fulton Dr. LE67: Coal 7B 34
Furlong Cl. DE13: Alre 7D 24
Furlong La. DE13: Alre 7D 24
Furnace La. DE12: Moi 6B 30
Furnace La. Ind. Est. DE12: Moi 6B 30
Furrows Dr. DE13: Bur T 6F 9
Fyfield Rd. DE15: Stap 2K 19

G

Gables, The DE11: New 3F 21
  LE65: Ash Z 5B 32
Gainsborough Way DE15: Win 4C 14
Galahad Dr. DE13: Stre 4K 9
Gallows La. DE12: Mea 7H 37
Gamble Cl. LE67: Ibs 5B 40
Garden, The DE65: Rep 4K 11
Garden La. LE67: Ibs 7B 40
Garden Rd. LE67: Coal 7F 35
Garendon Rd. LE67: Coal 2J 41
Garfield Rd. LE67: Hug 3D 40
Garganey Cl. LE67: Coal 2H 41
Garrett Sq. DE13: Rol D 2H 9
Gartan Rd. DE14: Bran 7F 13
Gatcombe Cl. DE13: Stre 5J 9
Gatcombe Dr. LE67: Coal 2H 41
Gawain Gro. DE13: Stre 4K 9
Geary Cl. LE67: Whit 4E 34
Geary La. DE15: Bret 6G 15
Gee Rd. LE67: Coal 7F 35
Gelsmoor Rd. LE67: Cole 1A 34
Genista Cl. DE15: Stap 7B 14
George Holmes Bus. Pk. DE11: Swad . .4H 21
George Holmes Way DE11: Swad 5H 21
George Newberry Pl. DE11: Chu G 6J 21
George Orton Ct. DE14: Bur T 2H 13
George Smith Dr. LE67: Coal 1E 40
George St. DE11: Chu G 6H 21
  DE14: Bur T 4J 13
  LE67: Whit 5G 35
George Walker Ct. DE14: Bur T 2H 13
Gerard Gro. DE65: Etw 1D 6
Gillamore Dr. LE67: Whit 7H 35
Gilmour La. DE13: Bar N 7H 17
Gisborne Cl. DE13: Yox 1B 16
Gladstone St. LE67: Ibs 7B 40
Glamis Cl. DE13: Stre 6J 9
Glamorgan Way DE11: Chu G 7G 21
Glebe, The DE12: Ros 3H 27
Glebe Cl. DE12: Cot E 6H 27
  DE13: Rol D 2F 9
Glebe Rd. LE67: Thri 1D 34
Glebe St. DE11: Swad 5J 21
Glebe Vw. LE67: Coal 7A 34
Glenalmond Cl. LE65: Ash Z 2K 31
Glen Av. LE67: Ibs 7C 40
Glencroft Cl. DE14: Bran 1G 19
Gleneagles Dr. DE13: Stre 5H 9
Glenfield Ri. DE13: Bur T 7F 9
Glen Ri. DE13: Bur T 7F 9
Glensyl Way DE14: Bur T 3K 13

Glen Way LE67: Coal 3G 41
Gloucester Way DE15: Stap 6C 14
Golding Cres. DE14: Bur T 1A 14
Goliath Rd. LE67: Coal 7E 34
Goodman St. DE14: Bur T 2J 13
Goodwood Cl. DE13: Stre 5H 9
Gordon St. DE14: Bur T 3H 13
Gorse La. DE12: Moi 3B 30
Gorse Rd. LE67: Hug 4D 40
Gorsey Leys DE12: Ove 6K 29
Gorsty Leys DE65: Fin 4K 7
Goseley Av. DE11: Hart 4D 22
Goseley Cres. DE11: Hart 4D 22
GOSELEY DALE **3D 22**
Gough Side DE14: Bur T 5J 13
Gracedieu LE67: Whit 1G 35
Grace Dieu Rd. LE67: Whit 2E 34
Grafton Cl. DE15: Stap 6C 14
Graham Cl. DE14: Bran 1H 19
Grain Warehouse Yd. DE14: Bur T 4H 13
Granary Wharf Bus. Pk. DE14: Bur T 2K 13
Grange, The DE14: Bur T 4G 13
   LE65: Pac .7B 32
Grange Cl. DE14: Bur T 3G 13
                           (not continuous)
   LE65: Ash Z 4K 31
Grange Ct. DE65: Egg 1C 10
Grange Farm Bus. Pk. LE67: Hug 5F 41
Grange Farm Ct. DE12: Lin 2D 28
Grange Nature Reserve **2C 40**
Grange Rd. DE11: New 3F 21
   LE67: Bar H, Hug 4E 40
   LE67: Ibs .7B 40
Grange St. DE14: Bur T 4G 13
Grangewood Gdns. DE12: Lin 3E 28
Grants Yd. DE14: Bur T 4H 13
Grants Yd. Bldgs. *DE14: Bur T* *4H 13*
                           (off Grants Yd.)
Granville Cl. DE65: Hatt 4C 4
Granville Cft. DE11: Mid 3B 22
Granville Ind. Est. DE11: Wood 6A 22
Granville St. DE11: Wood 5B 22
Granville St. DE11: Wood 5B 22
Granville Way DE11: Swad 4A 22
Grasmere LE67: Coal 7J 35
Grasmere Cl. DE15: Stap 6C 14
Grassy La. DE12: Mea 4G 37
Graycar Bus. Pk. DE13: Bar N 7A 18
Great Furlong DE13: Alre 7D 24
Green, The DE12: Don 1B 36
   DE13: Bar N 7F 17
   DE13: Stre 5K 9
   DE15: Bret 4H 15
   DE65: W'ton 7H 7
                           (not continuous)
   LE65: Ash Z 3A 32
   LE67: Don H 5D 40
   LE67: Thri 2E 34
Greenacre Pk. DE12: Cot E 6H 27
Greenacres LE67: Coal 1J 41
Green Bank Leisure Cen. **4J 21**
Green Cl. DE65: W'ton 7H 7
Green Ends La. DE65: Scro 5A 4
Greenfield Dr. DE12: Lin 3D 28
Greenfield Rd. DE12: Mea 5G 37
Greenfields Dr. LE67: Coal 1H 41
GREENHILL **2H 41**
Greenhill Rd. LE67: Coal 1H 41
Greenhouse Gardening & Environmental Centre, The
. . . . **5A 14**
Greenlands DE11: Mid 1J 21
Green La. DE12: Ove 5G 29
   DE13: Bar N, Wych 4E 24
   DE13: Bur T 7G 9
   DE13: Tut .1B 8
   DE65: Burn 1G 7
   LE67: Whit 7F 35
Greenline Bus. Pk. DE14: Bur T 4G 13
Greenmount St. DE11: Chu G 7G 21
Greenside Cl. DE12: Don 1B 36
Greensmith Cl. DE15: Win 4D 14
Green St. DE14: Bur T 6J 13
Greenvale Cl. DE15: Stap 7A 14
Green Valley Dr. DE13: Bur T 6F 9
Greenway DE15: Win 3B 14
Greenwich Av. DE11: Chu G 7F 21
Greenwood Rd. DE15: Stap 7K 13
Gregson Cl. DE11: Swad 3J 21
Gresley Office Pk. DE11: Swad 5F 21
Gresley Woodlands DE11: Chu G 6H 21
Gresley Wood Rd. DE11: Chu G, Swad 5G 21
Gretton Av. DE13: Stre 5K 9
Griffith Gdns. LE65: Ash Z 4J 31
Grindley Way DE11: Wood 7C 22
Grizedale Cl. DE15: Stap 6C 14
Grove, The DE13: Tate 7A 12
Grove M. DE13: Bar N 7H 17
Grove Pk. DE65: Etw 3C 6
Grove Rd. LE67: Whit 5F 35

Grove St. DE11: Swad 4J 21
Grunmore Dr. DE13: Stre 4K 9
Guildford Av. DE11: Mid 2B 22
Guildhall Cl. DE11: Chu G 7F 21
Guild St. DE14: Bur T 4J 13
Guinevere Av. DE13: Stre 4K 9
Gunby Hill DE12: Neth 7G 29
Guscott Rd. LE67: Coal 1F 41
Gutteridge St. LE67: Coal 1D 40

H

Hackett Cl. LE65: Ash Z 2A 32
Hadley End DE13: Yox 6A 16
Hadley St. DE13: Yox 1A 16
Hailebury Av. LE65: Ash Z 2K 31
Halcyon Ct. DE14: Bur T 3G 13
Halcyon Way DE14: Bur T 3G 13
Halifax Cl. DE65: Hilt 3K 5
Hallams Row DE14: Bur T 3H 13
Hall Cl. DE11: Blac 1F 31
Hallcroft Av. DE12: Ove 6J 29
Hall Farm Cl. DE11: Swad 4K 21
Hall Farm Rd. DE11: Swad 4K 21
Hallfields Rd. DE15: Stan 4D 20
Hall Gdns. LE67: Rav 2F 39
Hall Gate LE67: Coal 2K 41
Hall Grn. Av. DE13: Stre 4K 9
Hall Grounds DE13: Rol D 2F 9
Hall La. DE12: Don 2B 36
   DE65: W'ton 1J 11
   LE65: Pac .7A 32
   LE67: Whit 5G 35
Hall Rd. DE13: Rol D 2E 8
Hall St. DE11: Chu G 6H 21
   LE67: Ibs .7A 40
Hall Wood Cl. DE11: Chu G 6H 21
Hamble Way DE65: Hilt 4H 5
Hamilton Dr. DE11: Swad 3K 21
Hamilton Flds. DE15: Bur T 5B 14
Hamilton Gro. DE11: Swad 3A 22
Hamilton Rd. DE15: Bur T 5B 14
   LE67: Coal 2K 41
Hamilton Ter. DE65: W'ton 1J 11
Hampton Cl. LE67: Coal 2G 41
Hanbury Av. DE65: Hatt 4C 4
Hanbury Rd. DE13: Ans 1A 12
Hanchurch Cl. DE15: Win 3B 14
Handsacre Cl. DE11: Swad 5G 21
Hapden Ho. DE15: Stap 2K 19
Harbin Rd. DE12: Wal T 7C 18
Harbury St. DE13: Bur T 1F 13
Harcourt Rd. DE14: Bran 7D 12
Hardy Cl. DE13: Bar N 2H 25
Harebell Cl. DE11: Wood 4B 22
Harehedge La.
   DE13: Bur T 6G 9
Hargate Rd. DE15: Stap 6D 14
Harker Dr. LE67: Coal 3H 41
Harlaxton St. DE13: Bur T 1F 13
Harlech Way DE13: Stre 6J 9
Harley's Ct. DE12: Ove 5J 29
Harper Av. DE13: Bur T 7H 9
Harper Ct. DE13: Bur T 7H 9
Harratts Cl. LE67: Ibs 7B 40
Harrison Cl. DE14: Bran 7G 13
Harrison Ct. DE65: Hatt 5K 5
Harrison Pl. LE67: Coal 2D 40
Harrow Cl. LE65: Ash Z 1K 31
Harrow Dr. DE14: Bur T 7H 13
Harrow Rd. DE11: Mid 1J 21
Hartshill Rd. DE11: Hart 4D 22
HARTSHORNE **1D 22**
Hartshorne Rd. DE11: Wood 5C 22
Harvest Gro. DE12: Moi 4D 30
Harvest Hill DE11: Mid 1J 21
Harwood Av. DE14: Bran 7D 12
Haslyn Wlk. LE67: Coal 2J 41
                           (not continuous)
Hassall Rd. DE65: Hatt 4C 4
Hastings, The LE67: Ibs 6B 40
Hastings Av. LE67: Whit 5H 35
Hastings Hollow DE12: Mea 6F 37
Hastings Rd. DE11: Swad 5J 21
Hastings Way LE65: Ash Z 4B 32
HATTON **5C 4**
HATTON FIELDS **1D 4**
Hawfield La. DE15: Win 4C 14
                           (North St.)
   DE15: Win 3E 14
                           (Osprey Cl.)
Hawkins La. DE14: Bur T 3J 13
Hawkins La. Ind. Est. *DE14: Bur T* *2K 13*
                           (off Wharf Rd.)
Hawk's Ct. DE15: Win 4E 14
Hawksley Dr. DE13: Rol D 2G 9
Hawley Cl. LE67: Hug 4F 41

Hawthorn Cl. DE65: Hilt 4J 5
   LE67: Coal 1F 41
Hawthorn Cres. DE15: Stap 1A 20
Hawthorne Cl. DE12: Mea 4F 37
Hawthorn Gro. DE13: Tut 6B 4
Hawthorn Ri. DE11: New 4K 7
Haydock Cl. DE14: Bran 1F 19
Hayes, The DE65: Fin 4K 7
Hayes Cl. LE67: Whit 5G 35
Hays, The DE65: Hatt 3B 4
Hay Wain La. DE11: Mid 1J 21
Hay Wlk. DE14: Bur T 5K 13
Hay Wharf Rd. *DE14: Bur T* *4K 13*
                           (off Bridge St.)
Haywoods Rd. DE11: Wood 7B 22
Hazel Cl. DE11: New, Swad 3H 21
   DE12: Mea 5F 37
Hazel Gro. DE12: Moi 3E 30
Hazelwood Rd. DE15: Stap 2K 19
HCM Ind. Est. DE14: Bur T 3K 13
Headingley Cl. LE67: Coal 3H 41
Headstock Cl. LE67: Coal 7C 34
Hearthcote Rd. DE11: Swad 6G 21
Hearthcote Rd. Ind. Est. DE11: Swad 4H 21
Heath End La. LE65: Calke, Smis 4K 23
HEATHER **7H 39**
Heather Cl. DE14: Bran 7F 13
Heatherdale LE67: Ibs 7A 40
Heather Ho. LE67: Hea 7G 39
Heather La. LE65: Pac 1B 38
   LE67: Nor H 4E 38
   LE67: Rav .5J 39
Heathfield LE67: Thri 1F 35
Heathlands Grange DE15: Stap 1K 19
Heath La. DE11: Blac 7F 23
                           (not continuous)
   DE65: Fin .5K 7
   LE65: Smis 5G 23
Heathley M. DE14: Bur T 7H 13
Heath Rd. DE15: Stap 1K 19
Heathway DE65: Hatt 5B 4
Hector Rd. LE67: Coal 7E 34
Hedge Gro. DE11: Mid 1J 21
Hedge Rd. LE67: Hug 3D 40
Helmsdale Cl. LE67: Coal 1K 41
Helston Cl. DE12: Lin 4E 28
Hendeley Ct. DE14: Bur T 4F 13
Henhurst Farm DE13: Bur T 2C 12
Henhurst Hill DE13: Ans, Bur T 3A 12
Henhurst Ridge DE13: Bur T 3B 12
Henley Gro. DE11: Chu G 6F 21
Henson's La. LE67: Thri 1E 34
Hepworth Rd. DE11: Blac, Wood 6D 22
Herbert St. DE15: Win 4C 14
Hereford Cres. DE11: Mid 2A 22
Heritage Cl. DE11: Swad 5K 21
Heritage Way DE15: Stap 6B 14
Hermitage Ct. LE67: Whit 6F 35
Hermitage Golf Course **5F 35**
Hermitage Ind. Estate, The LE67: Coal 7D 34
Hermitage Leisure Cen. **5F 35**
Hermitage Pk. Way DE11: New 1H 21
Hermitage Rd. LE67: Whit 6E 34
Heron Cl. DE13: Alre 7D 24
Heron Dr. DE11: Wood 5C 22
Heron Way LE67: Coal 2G 41
Hervey Woods LE67: Whit 4F 35
Hevea Rd. DE15: Win 1H 13
Hextall Dr. LE67: Ibs 7B 40
Higgins Rd. DE11: New 2G 21
Higgott Cl. DE14: Bran 7F 13
High Bank Rd. DE15: Win 4C 14
Highcroft Dr. DE14: Bur T 3E 12
High Cross DE11: Cas G 1F 29
HIGH CROSS BANK **1F 29**
Highfield Cl. DE13: Bur T 7F 9
Highfield Dr. DE15: Win 4A 14
Highfield Rd. DE11: Swad 5J 21
Highfields Cl. DE12: Lin 3D 28
   LE65: Ash Z 3J 31
   LE67: Nor H 4E 38
Highfield St. DE11: Swad 5J 21
   LE67: Coal 3C 40
Highgate LE65: Ash Z 1K 31
Highgrove Cl. DE13: Stre 5J 9
Highland Cl. LE67: Coal 2G 41
Highlands Dr. DE15: Win 3B 14
High St. DE11: New 2G 21
   DE11: Swad 4K 21
   DE11: Wood 5C 22
   DE12: Lin .4C 28
   DE12: Mea 6F 37
   DE13: Tut .7B 4
   DE14: Bur T 5J 13
   DE65: Rep 4K 11
   LE65: Pac .7B 32
   LE67: Coal 1D 40
   LE67: Ibs .7B 40
Hilary Cres. LE67: Whit 6H 35

Hillcrest DE13: Tut 1A 8
Hillcrest Av. DE15: Win 3B 14
Hillfield La. DE13: Stre 5K 9
Hill Ri. DE12: Mea .4F 37
Hillsdale Rd. DE15: Win 2C 14
Hillside DE13: Tut .7A 4
    DE65: Fin 4K 7
Hillside Gdns. DE11: Chu G 6G 21
Hillside Rd. DE11: Cas G 3D 28
    DE12: Lin 3D 28
Hill St. DE11: New 2G 21
    DE11: Swad 5K 21
    DE12: Don 1B 36
    DE15: Stap 1K 19
    LE65: Ash Z 3K 31
Hilltop Ind. Est.
    LE67: Bar H 6K 41
HILTON 3J 5
Hilton Bus. Pk. DE65: Hilt 5K 5
Hilton Cl. DE11: New 1H 21
Hilton Rd. DE65: Egg 6B 6
    DE65: Etw 1C 6
Hobart Cl. DE15: Win 5D 14
Hockley, The LE67: Whit 4G 35
Hogarth Rd. LE67: Whit 4G 35
Holcombe Cl. LE67: Whit 3F 35
Holdings, The DE11: Chu G 7H 21
Holdon Cft. DE12: Ros 3H 27
Holland Cl. LE67: Whit 4F 35
Holland Pk. DE13: Bar N 6H 17
Hollies Cl. DE15: New S 6F 11
Hollow, The LE67: Nor H 4E 38
Hollow Cres. DE15: Win 3D 14
Hollow La. DE15: Win 3D 14
Hollows, The DE15: Stap 6A 14
Holly Bank LE67: Hug 4E 40
Holly Bank Cl. DE11: New 1H 21
Holly Cl. DE12: Moi 3E 30
Holly Ct. DE11: Wood 6C 22
Holly Grn. DE15: Stap 7A 14
Holly Hayes Rd. LE67: Whit 5G 35
Hollyhock Way DE14: Bran 1D 18
Holly Rd. DE12: Mea 5F 37
    DE13: Bar N 7G 17
Hollys Rd. DE13: Yox 2A 16
Holly St. DE15: Stap 7A 14
Holme Cl. DE65: Hatt 4B 4
Holme Farm Av. DE15: Stap 7A 14
Holmes Cl. DE11: Swad 3K 21
    LE67: Hug 4E 40
Holts La. DE13: Tut 1A 8
    LE67: Don H 4C 40
Holyoake Cres. LE67: Hea 7H 39
Holyoake Dr. LE67: Hea 7H 39
Holywell Av. LE65: Ash Z 2A 32
Homecroft Dr. LE65: Pac 7A 32
Home Farm Ct. DE11: Cas G 7E 20
Home Farm Pk. DE13: Rol D 2F 9
Homestead Rd. LE67: Thri 1E 34
Honeysuckle Cl. DE11: New 2H 21
    LE67: Coal 2H 41
Honeysuckle Vw. DE15: Stap 7B 14
Hood Ct. LE65: Ash Z 3A 32
    (off North St.)
Hood Park Leisure Cen. 2A 32
HOON 2D 4
HOON HAY 5D 4
Hoon La. DE65: Hilt 2F 5
HOON RIDGE 2F 5
Hoon Ridge DE65: Hilt 1F 5
Hoon Rd. DE65: Hatt 5C 4
Hope Way DE11: Chu G 7F 21
Hopley Rd. DE13: Ans 2A 12
Hopmeadow Way DE15: Stap 6B 14
Hopwood La. DE14: Bur T 1A 14
Hornbrook Cl. DE13: Bur T 6G 9
Hornbrook Rd. DE13: Bur T 7G 9
HORNINGLOW 7H 9
Horninglow Cft. DE13: Bur T 1H 13
Horninglow Rd. DE14: Bur T 1H 13
Horninglow Rd. Nth. DE13: Bur T 7G 9
Horninglow St. DE14: Bur T 3J 13
Hornton Rd. DE13: Bur T 7G 9
Horseshoe Cl. LE67: Ibs 6A 40
Horses La. DE12: Mea 6G 37
Horton Av. DE13: Stre 7A 10
Hospital La. LE67: Rav 2K 39
    LE67: Swan 2C 34
Hotel St. LE67: Coal 1E 40
Hough Hill LE67: Swan 6B 34
Howden Cl. DE11: New 3H 21
Howe Cl. LE67: Whit 4E 34
Howe Rd. LE67: Whit 4E 34
HUGGLESCOTE 4E 40
Hull St. DE65: Hilt 4K 5
Humber St. DE65: Hilt 4H 5
Hunter St. DE14: Bur T 4H 13
Huntingdon Ct. DE12: Mea 5D 36
    LE65: Ash Z 3A 32

Huntingdon Rd. DE15: Stap 1J 19
    LE65: Ash Z 4J 31
Huntingdon Way DE12: Mea 5D 36
Huntspill Rd. DE65: Hilt 4K 5
Hunt Way DE11: Swad 4B 22
Hurst Dr. DE13: Stre 5K 9
Hylton Cl. DE14: Bran 1F 19

I

IBSTOCK 7A 40
Ibstock Cotts. DE12: Mea 7G 37
Ibstock Ind. Est. LE67: Ibs 6C 40
Ibstock Leisure Complex 7B 40
    (off Central Av.)
Ibstock Rd. LE67: Ell 7D 40
    LE67: Rav 4A 40
Ibstock St. DE13: Bur T 1G 13
Imex Bus. Pk. DE14: Bur T 4G 13
Inge Dr. DE12: Alre 7D 24
Ingleby Cl. DE11: Swad 5G 21
Ingle Dr. LE65: Ash Z 2J 31
Ingles Hill Caravan Site LE65: Ash Z 1H 31
Interlink Pk. LE67: Bar H 7J 41
Interlink Way E. LE67: Bar H 7J 41
Interlink Way Sth. LE67: Bar H 7H 41
Interlink Way W. LE67: Bar H 7H 41
Ironwalls La. DE13: Tut 1B 8
Isis Way DE65: Hilt 4K 5
Island Cl. DE11: Alb V 1K 29
Ivanhoe Bus. Pk. LE65: Ash Z 7K 23
Ivanhoe Dr. LE65: Ash Z 3J 31
Ivanhoe Ind. Est. LE65: Ash Z 1K 31
    (not continuous)
Ivanhoe Pk. Way LE65: Ash Z 7K 23
Ivanhoe Way DE12: Moi 6C 30
    LE65: Ash Z 2B 32
Iveagh Cl. DE12: Mea 5G 37
Ivy Cl. DE12: Don .1B 36
    DE65: W'ton 1H 11
Ivy Ct. DE65: Egg .1B 10
    DE65: Etw 1C 6
    DE65: Hilt 4J 5
Ivy Gro. DE13: Bur T 7H 9
Ivy Lodge Cl. DE15: Stap 1K 19

J

Jacklin Cl. DE14: Bran 2F 19
Jackson Av. DE13: Stre 7A 10
Jackson Cl. DE12: Ove 6J 29
Jacksons La. DE65: Etw 3D 6
Jackson St. LE67: Coal 1D 40
Jacks Wlk. LE67: Hug 3C 40
Jacobean Cl. DE15: Win 3D 14
Jacquemart Cl. LE67: Coal 1K 41
    (off Romans Cres.)
Jacques St. LE67: Ibs 6B 40
James Brindley Way DE13: Stre 5A 10
James Ct. DE14: Bur T 5J 13
    (off Ordish Ct.)
James St. DE11: Mid 3A 22
    DE14: Bur T 5H 13
    LE67: Coal 2D 40
Jarvis Way LE67: Whit 4F 35
Jasmine Cl. DE15: Stap 7B 14
Jeffcoats La. LE67: Swan 3C 34
Jenkins Rd. LE67: Coal 1F 41
Jennings Way DE14: Bur T 4F 13
Jenny's La. LE67: Rav 2A 40
Jephson Cl. DE14: Bran 1G 19
Jeque Pl. DE13: Bur T 7J 9
Jerram's La. DE15: Stap 7K 13
Jewsbury Av. DE12: Mea 5G 37
Jinny Cl. DE65: Hatt 5B 4
John Port Cl. DE65: Etw 1D 6
Johnson Cl. LE67: Thri 1E 34
Johnson's Cotts. DE12: Mea 5F 37
    (off Navigation St.)
John St. DE11: Chu G 6K 21
    DE11: New 2F 21
    DE11: Swad 3J 21
    LE67: Thri 2E 34
Jordan Av. DE13: Stre 4A 10
Jubilee Cotts. DE13: Ans 7B 8
Jubilee Cft. LE67: Swep 7C 38
Jubilee Pk. DE11: Wood 4C 22
Jubilee Ri. DE15: Win 4D 14
    (off Canterbury Rd.)
Jubilee Ter. DE12: Don 1B 36

K

Kane Cl. LE67: Coal 1C 40
Kay Cl. LE67: Coal 2J 41
Kay Dr. DE11: New 3G 21

Keats Dr. DE11: Swad 2K 21
Keble Cl. DE15: Stap 5D 14
Kedleston Cl. DE13: Stre 5H 9
Keele Dr. DE11: Chu G 7F 21
Keepers Cl. DE12: Moi 5D 30
Kelham Gro. LE67: Rav 2K 39
Kelso Cl. DE12: Mea 4F 37
    LE65: Ash Z 3B 32
Kelso Ct. LE67: Thri 1F 35
Kemp Rd. LE67: Coal 3D 40
Kempton Rd. DE15: Win 4B 14
Kendal Pl. LE67: Ell 6E 40
Kendal Rd. LE67: Ell 6E 40
Kendrick Cl. LE67: Coal 7C 34
Kendricks Cl. DE11: Hart 1D 22
Kenilworth Av. DE13: Stre 7J 9
Kenilworth Dr. LE65: Ash Z 4B 32
Kenmore Cres. LE67: Coal 1K 41
Kensington Rd. DE15: Win 4B 14
    LE67: Coal 2H 41
Kent Rd. DE15: Stap 2K 19
Kent Way DE11: Chu G 6F 21
Kestrel Av. DE11: Wood 5C 22
Kestrel Way DE15: Win 4D 14
Kilburn Way DE11: New 3G 21
Kiln Cft. DE65: Etw 1D 6
Kiln Way DE11: Wood 5A 22
Kilwardby St. LE65: Ash Z 3K 31
Kimberley Dr. DE15: Win 4D 14
Kinder Av. DE11: New 3H 21
King Edward VII Community College Sports Hall
    . . . . .6K 35
King Edward Pl. DE14: Bur T 4G 13
Kingfisher Av. DE11: Wood 5C 22
Kingfisher Cl. LE67: Whit 7J 35
King George Av. LE65: Ash Z 2K 31
King John's Rd. LE67: Whit 3G 35
King Richard's Hill LE67: Whit 4G 35
King Richard Way LE65: Ash Z 2C 32
King's Bromley Rd. DE13: Alre 7B 24
Kingsbury Cl. DE15: Win 3B 14
Kingsdale Cft. DE13: Stre 6J 9
Kingsley Rd. DE14: Bur T 7J 9
Kingsmead DE13: Stre 6K 9
Kings Rd. DE11: Swad 3J 21
Kingston Rd. DE15: Win 5D 14
King St. DE13: Yox 1B 16
    DE14: Bur T 7H 13
    LE67: Coal 2E 40
Kingsway DE14: Bran 7G 13
Kinver Rd. DE15: Win 3B 14
Kirkhill Cl. LE67: Coal 1K 41
Kirkland Cl. LE65: Ash Z 3A 32
Kirkland Way DE11: Chu G 7J 21
Kirton Rd. LE67: Coal 1K 41
Kitling Greaves La. DE14: Bur T 6F 9
Knightsbridge Way DE13: Stre 7J 9
Knights Cl. LE65: Ash Z 2K 31
Knights Ct. DE13: Stre 5K 9
Knight's Gth. LE67: Whit 4G 35
Knight's La. DE15: Bret, Rep 4H 15
    DE65: Rep 4H 15
Knights Pl. DE15: Bret 5E 14
Knob Flds. DE11: Cas G 1F 29
Knoll, The DE11: Mid 2J 21
Knowles Hill DE13: Rol D 3G 9
Knowles Vw. DE11: Swad 4A 22
Koppe Cl. DE12: Moi 3E 30
Kyle Rd. DE65: Hilt 5J 5

L

Laburnum Rd. DE11: New 2H 21
    DE15: Stap 2A 20
Laburnum Way DE65: Etw 2D 6
Ladle End La. DE12: Wal T 7C 18
Ladybower Cl. DE11: Swad 6H 21
Ladyfields DE11: Mid 2A 22
Ladyfields Way DE11: New 2G 21
Ladywell Cl. DE13: Stre 5K 9
Lagoona Pk. DE12: Ove 6K 29
Lakeshore Cres. LE67: Whit 5F 35
Lakeside Vw. LE67: Whit 6F 35
Lakins, The DE12: Mea 5G 37
Lancaster Cl. LE67: Coal 1K 41
Lancaster Dr. DE13: Tut 1A 8
    DE65: Hilt 3K 5
Lancelot Dr. DE13: Stre 5K 9
Langer Cl. DE14: Bran 2F 19
Langton Cl. LE67: Whit 3F 35
Lansdowne Rd. DE11: Swad 5H 21
    DE14: Bran 1E 18
Lansdowne Ter. DE14: Bur T 2J 13
Lapley Dr. DE13: Stre 6K 9
Larch Rd. DE11: New 1G 21
Larkin Cl. DE11: Swad 5J 21
Latham Cl. DE15: Stap 5D 14
Latham Ho. DE65: Rep 4J 11

Lathkill Dale DE11: Chu G 6G 21
Laud Cl. LE67: Ibs 7A 40
Launceston Dr. LE67: Hug 3D 40
Laurel Cotts. DE13: Ans 7B 8
  (off Main Rd.)
Laurel Gro. DE15: Stap 3K 19
Lavender Cl. DE14: Bran 7F 13
Lavender Wlk. LE67: Cole 1G 33
Lawn Av. DE65: Etw 1D 6
Lawns, The DE13: Rol D 2F 9
Lawns Dr. DE11: New 1H 21
Lawnswood Cl. DE65: Etw 1D 6
Lawrence Cl. LE67: Ell 6D 40
Leamington Rd. DE14: Bran 1D 18
Leander Ri. DE15: Stap 7A 14
Leascroft, The LE67: Rav 2K 39
Leawood Rd. DE11: Mid 1A 22
Leedhams Cft. DE12: Wal T 1C 26
Lees Cres. LE67: Whit 4H 35
Legion Dr. LE67: Ibs 7B 40
Leicester Rd. DE12: Mea 5G 37
  LE65: Ash Z, Pac 3B 32
  LE67: Ibs .....6B 40 & 7D 40
  LE67: Rav 6H 33
    (Ashby Rd.)
  LE67: Rav 2K 39
    (Ravenslea)
  LE67: Whit 5G 35
Leicester St. DE14: Bur T 7H 13
Leith Cl. LE65: Ash Z 4C 32
Lemon Gro. DE11: Chu G 7J 21
Lewis Dr. DE13: Bur T 7G 9
Lewisham Dr. LE67: Chu G 7F 21
Leyburn Cl. DE11: Chu G 7J 21
Ley Cft. DE65: Hatt 4B 4
Leyfields Farm M. DE13: Ans 1B 12
Leys, The DE11: New 3F 21
Leys Ct. DE11: New 2F 21
Lichfield Av. DE11: Mid 3B 22
Lichfield Rd. DE13: Bar N 1J 25
  DE14: Bran 1J 25
Lichfield St. DE14: Bur T 6J 13
Lightoaks Cl. DE14: Bur T 1K 13
Lightwood Rd. DE13: Yox 3A 16
Lilac Gro. DE12: Stap 2A 20
Lillehammer Dr. LE67: Coal 2E 40
Lily Bank LE67: Thri 1D 34
Limby Hall La. LE67: Swan 3A 34
Lime Av. DE12: Mea 4F 37
Lime Ct. DE15: Stap 1K 19
Lime Gro. DE15: Stap 2K 19
  DE65: Hatt 3C 4
Limes, The DE11: Hart 2E 22
  DE15: Win 5D 14
  LE67: Rav 7B 34
Limestone Cl. DE11: Hart 5C 22
Limetree Av. DE11: Mid 1J 21
Lincoln Rd. DE15: Stap 1J 19
Lincoln Way DE11: Mid 3B 22
Lincote Way DE11: Wood 7B 22
Linden Cl. LE67: Ibs 6A 40
Linden Rd. DE13: Bar N 7G 17
Linden Way LE67: Coal 7D 34
Linford Cres. LE67: Coal 1J 41
Lingfield Rd. DE14: Bran 1E 18
Links Cl. LE67: Hug 4E 40
LINTON 3E 28
LINTON HEATH 4F 29
Linton Heath DE12: Lin 4F 29
Linton Rd. DE11: Cas G 2F 29
  DE12: Cald, Ros 4J 27
LITTLE BURTON 2H 13
Lit. Burton E. Bur T 2J 13
Lit. Burton W. DE14: Bur T 3J 13
Little Cl. DE11: Swad 3J 21
Lit. Derby Hill DE65: Burn 3J 7
Little La. LE65: Pac 7A 32
Little Liverpool DE12: Cot E 7H 27
Lit. Thorn Ind. Est. DE11: Wood 6C 22
Locksley Cl. LE65: Ash Z 2K 31
Lockton Cl. LE65: Ash Z 2B 32
Lodge Cl. DE65: Etw 1D 6
  LE65: Ash Z 4K 31
Lodge Hill DE13: Tut 3D 8
Lohengrin Ct. DE13: Stre 4K 9
Loire Cl. LE65: Ash Z 2K 31
London Rd. LE67: Coal 1E 40
Longbow Cl. DE13: Stre 5G 9
Longbow Gro. DE13: Stre 5H 9
Longcliff Rd. LE67: Coal 2J 41
Longcroft La. DE13: Yox 1B 16
Longfellow Cl. DE14: Bur T 7J 9
Longford Cl. DE15: Stap 5C 14
Longhedge La. DE13: Ans, Bur T 6D 8
Longlands DE65: Rep 7K 11
Longlands La. DE65: Fin 4K 7
Longlands Rd. DE11: Mid 1A 22
Long La. LE67: Coal 1F 41
  WS13: Frad 7B 24

Longmead Rd. DE13: Bur T 1H 13
Long St. DE15: Stap 1K 19
Lonsdale Rd. DE14: Bran 7G 13
Lords Cl. LE67: Coal 3H 41
Lordswell Rd. DE14: Bur T 3D 12
Lorne Dr. DE15: Win 4C 14
Loudoun Ct. LE65: Ash Z 3A 32
Loudoun Way LE65: Ash Z 4J 31
Loughborough Rd. LE67: Cole 2K 33
  LE67: Thri 2E 34
  LE67: Whit 3F 35
Lount La. DE13: Ans 5D 8
Lountside LE65: Ash Z 2D 32
Lovatt Cl. DE13: Stre 4A 10
Lovell Rd. DE15: Yox 3A 16
Lwr. Church St. LE65: Ash Z 3B 32
Lwr. High St. DE13: Tut 6B 4
LOWER MIDWAY 2A 22
Lwr. Moor Rd. LE67: Cole 1K 33
LOWER OUTWOODS 1E 12
Lwr. Outwoods Rd. DE13: Bur T 2E 12
Lwr. Packington Rd. LE65: Ash Z 4A 32
Loweswater Gro. LE65: Ash Z 5B 32
Lowman Way DE65: Hilt 5K 5
Lucas La. DE65: Hilt 3K 5
Lucepool La. DE13: Yox 4A 16
Ludgate St. DE13: Tut 7B 4
Lullington M. DE12: Ove 6H 29
Lullington Rd. DE12: Ove 6H 29
Luton Rd. DE11: Chu G 6F 21
Lyndham Av. DE15: Stap 6A 14
Lyne Ct. DE14: Bur T 4F 13
Lynmouth Ho. DE65: Hilt 4H 5
Lynwood Cl. DE14: Bran 1E 18
Lynwood Rd. DE14: Bran 1D 18

M

McAdam Cl. DE15: Stap 5C 14
McCarthy Cl. LE67: Whit 4F 35
Mackworth Cl. DE11: New 1J 21
Madras Rd. DE15: Win 4D 14
Magistrates' Court
  Burton upon Trent 3J 13
Main Line Ind. Est. DE14: Bur T 1K 13
Main Rd. DE13: Ans 1A 12
Main St. DE11: Blac 1E 30
  DE11: Chu G 6K 21
  DE11: Hart 1E 22
  DE11: New 2F 21
  DE12: Cald 2K 27
  DE12: Lin 3D 28
  DE12: Oak 3D 36
  DE12: Ove 6J 29
  DE12: Ros 3H 27
  DE12: Wal T 7B 18
  DE13: Alre 6C 24
  DE13: Ans 7B 8
  DE13: Bar N 6F 17
  DE13: Stre 5K 9
  DE13: Tate 7A 12
  DE13: Yox 2B 16
  DE14: Bran 1D 18
  DE15: New S 6F 11
  DE15: Stap 7K 13
  DE65: Burn 1H 7
  DE65: Egg 1C 10
  DE65: Etw 1C 6
  DE65: Hilt 3G 5
  DE65: Rep 7K 11
  LE65: Smis 5J 23
  LE67: Hea 7H 39
  LE67: Nor H 4E 38
  LE67: Rav 2K 39
  LE67: Swan 3C 34
  LE67: Swep 7B 38
  LE67: Thri 1E 34
Majolica M. DE11: Wood 6C 22
Mallard Cl. DE12: Mea 6E 36
Malmesbury Av. DE11: Mid 2A 22
Malthouse La. DE65: Fos 2C 4
Maltings, The DE14: Bur T 4H 13
  (off Grants Yd.)
  DE14: Bur T 3K 13
    (Glensyl Way)
  DE15: Stap 6B 14
Maltings Ind. Est. DE14: Bur T 1K 13
Maltsters, The DE14: Bur T 3K 13
Malvern Av. DE15: Stap 6A 14
Malvern Cres. LE65: Ash Z 1K 31
Malvern St. DE15: Stap 6A 14
Mammoth St. LE67: Coal 1E 40
Manchester La. DE11: Hart 2E 22
Mannings Ter. DE12: Mea 6F 37
Manor Brook Cl. LE67: Don H 5D 40
Manor Cl. DE15: Stan 2B 20
  LE65: Ash Z 4B 32

Manor Ct. DE13: Bar N 6G 17
Manor Cres. DE15: Stan 2B 20
Manor Cft. DE13: Tate 1K 17
  DE14: Bur T 5K 13
Manor Dr. DE14: Bur T 5K 13
Manor Flds. DE13: Alre 6C 24
Manor Ind. Est. DE14: Bur T 2K 13
Manor Rd. DE15: Stan 2B 20
  LE67: Don H 4D 40
  LE67: Hea 7G 39
Mnr. School Vw. DE12: Ove 6J 29
Manor Vw. DE11: Hart 2E 22
Mansfield Cl. DE11: Swad 4A 22
Mansfields Cft. DE65: Etw 1C 6
Mantle La. LE67: Coal 7D 34
Manton Cl. DE11: New 2G 21
  DE13: Stre 5A 10
Maple Ct. DE65: Rep 7K 11
  LE67: Bar H 5K 41
Maple Dr. LE67: Ibs 6A 40
Maple Gro. DE15: Stap 3K 19
Maple Rd. DE11: Mid 2J 21
Maple Way DE14: Bran 7E 12
Maplewell LE67: Coal 1J 41
Margaret St. LE67: Coal 1D 40
Marigold Pl. DE11: Wood 4C 22
Market Pl. DE14: Bur T 4H 13
  LE67: Whit 4G 35
Market St. DE11: Chu G 6J 21
  DE11: Swad 4J 21
  LE65: Ash Z 3A 32
  LE67: Coal 7D 34
Marlborough Ct. LE67: Coal 1D 40
Marlborough Cres. DE15: Stap 7A 14
Marlborough Sq. LE67: Coal 1D 40
Marlborough Way LE65: Ash Z 2K 31
Marlow Dr. DE14: Bran 7F 13
Marquis Ct. DE12: Moi 4B 30
Marquis Dr. DE12: Moi 4B 30
Marsden Cl. LE67: Rav 7A 34
Marston Brook DE65: Hilt 4K 5
Marston Cl. DE12: Moi 4D 30
Marston Cl. DE12: Moi 2F 9
  DE65: Hatt, Hilt, Rol D 5C 4
Marston Old La. DE65: Hatt 5C 4
MARSTON ON DOVE 5G 5
Marston Ri. DE15: Stap 7A 14
Marston's Vis. Cen. 4F 13
Marston Way LE67: Hea 7G 39
Martin Cl. LE67: Whit 3E 34
Martins Ct. LE67: Coal 7C 34
Maryland Dr. DE11: New 1H 21
Masefield Av. DE11: Mid 2K 21
Masefield Cl. DE12: Mea 7E 36
Masefield Cres. DE14: Bur T 1J 13
Mason Cres. DE11: Swad 4B 22
Matsyard Path DE11: New 1G 21
Matthews Ct. LE65: Ash Z 3J 31
Mayfair DE11: New 2F 21
Mayfield Dr. DE15: Stap 7B 14
Mayfield Rd. DE15: Win 4B 14
Maypole Hill DE11: Swad 2H 21
Mays Wlk. DE13: Alre 6C 24
Mead Cres. DE15: Stan 2B 20
Meadow Cl. DE65: Rep 7K 11
Meadow Ct. DE14: Bur T 4A 14
  (off Meadow Rd.)
Meadow Gdns. DE12: Mea 7F 37
Meadow La. DE11: New 3G 21
  (not continuous)
  DE13: Stre 6B 10
  DE13: Yox .....7A 16 & 3A 16
  LE67: Coal 1H 41
Meadow Rise DE13: Bar N 7H 17
Meadow Rd. DE14: Bur T 4A 14
Meadowside Dr. DE14: Bur T 4K 13
Meadowside Leisure Cen. 4K 13
Meadow Vw. DE13: Rol D 2H 9
  LE67: Don H 5D 40
Meadow Vw. Rd. DE11: New 3G 21
Meadow Wlk. LE67: Ibs 6B 40
Meadow Way DE11: New 2H 21
Mead Wlk. DE15: Stan 2B 20
Meakin Dr. DE11: Wood 7C 22
Mear Greaves La. DE15: Win 3C 14
Mease, The DE65: Hilt 4K 5
Mease Cl. DE12: Mea 6F 37
MEASHAM 5F 37
Measham Leisure Cen. 5F 37
Measham Mus. 6F 37
Measham Rd. DE12: Acre, Oak 4A 36
  DE12: App M 7C 36
  DE12: Don, Moi, Oak 6C 30
  (not continuous)
  LE65: Ash Z, Pac 2J 37
  (not continuous)
Mecca Bingo
  Burton upon Trent 4J 13
Melbourne Av. DE15: Win 4D 14

Melbourne Rd.—Oldfield Dr.

Melbourne Rd. LE67: Ibs 7A **40**
LE67: Rav 6K **39** & 5A **40**
Melbourne St. LE67: Coal 1D **40**
Mellor Dr. DE13: Alre 7C **24**
Mellor Rd. DE14: Bran 1F **19**
Melrose Cl. LE65: Ash Z 4C **32**
Melrose Rd. LE67: Thri 1E **34**
Melville Ct. DE65: Etw 2C **6**
Memorial Sq. LE67: Coal 1D **40**
Mendip Cl. LE65: Ash Z 4A **32**
Mercia Cl. DE65: Hatt 5C **4**
Mercia Ct. DE65: Rep 7K **11**
Mercia Dr. DE65: W'ton 1H **11**
Mercia Marina 6J **7**
Mercia Pk. DE14: Bur T 6E **12**
Meredith Cl. DE14: Bur T 1J **13**
Meredith Rd. LE65: Ash Z 2A **32**
Mereoak La. DE11: Hart 1H **23**
Merganser Way LE67: Coal 2H **41**
Merlin Cres. DE14: Bran 7E **12**
Merlin Way DE11: Wood 5C **22**
Merrydale Rd. DE15: Stap 7A **14**
Mersey Way DE65: Hilt 4K **5**
Merton Cl. DE11: Chu G 7F **21**
Mervyn Rd. DE15: Win 4B **14**
Messiter M. DE65: W'ton 1J **11**
Mewies Cl. DE12: Wal T 7C **18**
Mews, The DE14: Bur T 1H **19**
DE15: New S 7E **10**
Meynell Cl. DE15: Stap 6C **14**
Meynell St. DE11: Chu G 7H **21**
Mickleden Grn. LE67: Whit 7H **35**
Micklehome Dr. DE13: Alre 6E **24**
Mickleton Cl. DE11: Chu G 7J **21**
Middle Cl. DE11: Swad 4J **21**
Middleway Pk. DE14: Bur T 4K **13**
Middle Yard Leisure Pk. 4J **13**
Midland Grain Warehouse
DE14: Bur T 4H **13**
(off Borough Rd.)
Midland Rd. DE11: Swad 3J **21**
LE67: Ell, Hug 5D **40**
Midland Rd. Ind. Est.
DE11: Swad 4J **21**
MIDLANDS NHS TREATMENT CENTRE 2F **13**
MIDWAY 1K **21**
Midway Rd. DE11: Mid, Swad 3K **21**
Milford Dr. DE13: Stre 6A **10**
Mill Bank LE65: Ash Z 3A **32**
Mill Cl. DE11: Mid 3K **21**
DE15: New S 6F **11**
DE65: Fin 3K **7**
Mill Cres. DE13: Bar N 1H **25**
Mill Dam LE67: Hug 4E **40**
Mill End La. DE13: Alre 6C **24**
Millennium Av. DE12: Moi 4B **30**
Millersdale Cl. DE15: Win 2C **14**
Millers La. DE14: Bur T 4H **13**
Millers Wlk. LE67: Rav 3K **39**
Mill Farm La. LE65: Ash Z 5A **32**
Millfield Cl. LE65: Ash Z 1K **31**
Millfield Cft. DE11: Mid 1J **21**
Millfield St. DE11: Wood 6D **22**
Mill Fleam DE65: Hilt 4K **5**
Mill Grn. Cl. DE12: Cot E 6J **27**
Mill Hill DE65: Rep 7K **11**
Mill Hill Dr. DE15: Win 3C **14**
Mill Hill La. DE15: Win 3B **14**
Mill Ho. Cotts. *DE13: Ans* 7B **8**
(off Main St.)
MILLHOUSE ESTATE 1D **34**
Mill La. DE13: Bar N 1H **25**
DE65: Hilt 3H **5**
LE65: Ash Z 3A **32**
LE67: Cole 2B **34**
LE67: Hea 7H **39**
Mill Mdw. Way DE65: Etw 1C **6**
Mill Pond LE67: Hug 4E **40**
Mill Pond Cl. DE65: Hilt 3H **5**
Millpool Cl. DE11: Hart 1D **22**
Mill Stream La. DE13: Stre 5B **10**
Mill St. DE12: Cot E 6J **27**
LE65: Pac 7A **32**
Millway La. DE65: Burn 1H **7**
Milton Av. DE11: Mid 2K **21**
Milton Cl. DE12: Mea 7F **37**
Milton Ho. *DE14: Bur T* 4H **13**
(off Milton St.)
Milton Rd. DE65: Rep 6K **11**
Milton St. DE14: Bur T 5H **13**
Miry La. DE65: Fos 1B **4**
Mistletoe Dr. DE11: Wood 6C **22**
Mitchells Cl. DE65: Etw 1B **6**
Mitre, The DE65: Rep 4K **11**
Mitre Dr. DE65: Rep 4K **11**
Moat Bank DE15: Bret 5E **14**
Moat St. DE11: Chu G 7J **21**
MOIRA 5C **30**
Moira Furnace Mus. 6B **30**
Moira Rd. DE11: Wood 2A **30**
DE12: Don 1C **36**
DE12: Ove 6J **29**
LE65: Ash Z 3F **31**
Monarch Cl. DE13: Stre 6K **9**
Mona Rd. DE13: Bur T 2G **13**
Moncreiff Dr. DE13: Stre 5B **10**
Money Hill LE65: Ash Z 1A **32**
Monk St. DE13: Tut 7B **4**
Monsaldale Cl. DE15: Win 3C **14**
Monsom La. DE65: Rep 6K **11**
Montgomery Cl. DE65: Hilt 3K **5**
Montpelier Cl. DE14: Bran 1F **19**
Moor, The LE67: Cole 2K **33**
Moores Cl. DE13: Bur T 1G **13**
Moores Hill DE13: Tate 1K **17**
Moor Furlong DE13: Stre 5A **10**
Moorings, The DE13: Alre 6C **24**
Moorlands, The LE67: Cole 6J **33**
Moor La. LE67: Cole 3K **33**
Moor Rd. LE67: Ell 6F **41**
Moor St. DE14: Bur T 5H **13**
Moray Cl. DE11: Chu G 7G **21**
Moreton Ct. LE67: Coal 3E **40**
Morley Cl. DE15: Stap 5C **14**
Morley's Hill DE13: Bur T 7G **9**
Morley Wlk. DE11: Chu G 7F **21**
Morrey La. DE13: Yox 2A **16**
Morton Wlk. LE65: Ash Z 5J **31**
Mosley M. DE13: Rol D 2F **9**
Mosley St. DE14: Bur T 5H **13**
Mosley St. Bus. Pk. DE14: Bur T 4H **13**
Mossdale LE67: Whit 3F **35**
Mountbatten Cl. DE13: Stre 6J **9**
MOUNT PLEASANT 2F **29**
Mt. Pleasant Rd. DE11: Cas G 1F **29**
DE11: Chu G 7H **21**
DE65: Rep 7K **11**
Mount Rd. DE11: Cas G 1E **28**
DE11: Hart 4D **22**
DE15: Bret 4H **15**
Mount St. DE15: Win 4B **14**
Mount Wlk. LE65: Ash Z 3B **32**
Mulberry Way DE65: Hilt 3K **5**
Muscovey Rd. LE67: Coal 2H **41**
Mushroom La. DE11: Alb V 7K **21**
Musson Dr. LE65: Ash Z 4K **31**

N

Nankirks La. DE13: Ans 1A **12**
Napier Cl. DE11: Chu G 6F **21**
Napier St. DE14: Bur T 6H **13**
Narrow La. DE12: Don 2B **36**
Naseby Dr. LE65: Ash Z 2C **32**
National Brewery Centre, The 4J **13**
National Memorial Arboretum 7F **25**
National Memorial Arboretum Vis. Cen. 7F **25**
Navigation St. DE12: Mea 5F **37**
Needhams Wlk. LE67: Coal 1E **40**
Needwood Av. DE13: Rol D 2H **9**
Needwood Ct. DE13: Tut 7B **4**
Needwood Pk. DE13: Bar N 7G **17**
Needwood St. DE14: Bur T 4G **13**
Nelson Flds. LE67: Coal 7H **35**
Nelson Pl. LE65: Smis 5J **23**
Nelson Sq. *LE65: Smis* 5J **23**
(off Main St.)
Nelson St. DE11: Swad 3J **21**
DE15: Win 4D **14**
Nene Cl. DE13: Stre 5H **9**
Nene Way DE65: Hilt 4J **5**
LE67: Coal 3H **41**
Netherclose La. DE65: Scro 4A **4**
Nethercroft Dr. LE65: Pac 7B **32**
Netherhall Rd. DE11: Hart 1A **22**
Neville Cl. DE13: Rol D 3G **9**
Neville Dr. LE67: Coal 1H **41**
New Broadway LE67: Coal 1D **40**
Newbury Dr. DE13: Stre 5H **9**
Newby Cl. DE15: Stap 6C **14**
New Cl. LE67: Swan 5B **34**
Newfield Rd. DE15: Win 3C **14**
Newfields DE12: Moi 5C **30**
Newgatefield La. DE13: Ans 6C **8**
NEWHALL 2G **21**
Newhall Rd. DE11: Swad 3J **21**
Newhay DE13: Stre 5A **10**
New House DE65: Rep 4K **11**
Newlands Cl. DE11: Chu G 6H **21**
Newman Dr. DE11: Chu G 6F **21**
DE14: Bran 7G **13**
Newport Cl. DE14: Bur T 7J **9**
New Rd. DE11: New 2F **21**
DE11: Wood 6C **22**
DE12: Cot E 6J **27**
DE65: Hilt 3K **5**
LE67: Cole 1B **34**
New Row DE12: Moi 5D **30**
DE13: Tate 6A **12**
LE67: Ibs 7B **40**
New St. DE11: Chu G 6J **21**
DE12: Don 1B **36**
DE12: Mea, Oak 4E **36**
DE12: Oak 3D **36**
DE12: Ros 3J **27**
DE14: Bur T 5J **13**
LE67: Coal 2E **40**
NEW SWANNINGTON 4E **34**
Newton Cl. DE15: New S 6F **11**
Newton La. DE15: Bret, New S 6F **11**
Newton Leys DE15: Win 3D **14**
Newton M. DE15: Win 4A **14**
Newton Pk. DE15: New S 7E **10**
Newton Pk. Cl. DE11: New 1H **21**
Newton Rd. DE15: Bur T, New S 4A **14**
NEWTON SOLNEY 6F **11**
Nicklaus Cl. DE14: Bran 1F **19**
Nicolson Way DE14: Bur T 6F **13**
Nightingale Dr. DE11: Wood 5C **22**
Ninelands Mobile Home Pk. DE11: Hart 5D **22**
Ninth Av. DE14: Bur T 7D **12**
Noon Cft. DE13: Alre 7C **24**
Norfolk Rd. DE15: Stap 2J **19**
Normandy Rd. DE65: Hilt 3K **5**
Norman Keep DE13: Tut 7B **4**
Norman Rd. DE13: Tut 7B **4**
Norman Ter. *DE13: Stre* 4B **10**
(off Derby Rd.)
Normanton La. LE67: Hea 6G **39**
NORMANTON LE HEATH 4E **38**
Normanton Rd. LE65: Pac 1B **38**
NORRIS HILL 3E **30**
Norris Hill DE12: Moi 3E **30**
North Av. LE67: Coal 3E **40**
North Cl. DE11: Blac 1E **30**
DE65: W'ton 1J **11**
Northfield Dr. LE67: Coal 2H **41**
Northfield Rd. DE13: Bur T 7H **9**
Northfields LE65: Ash Z 1A **32**
Northside Bus. Pk. DE14: Bur T 1K **13**
North St. DE11: Swad 3J **21**
DE15: Win 4C **14**
LE65: Ash Z 3A **32**
LE67: Whit 4F **35**
Northumberland Rd. DE15: Stap 1J **19**
North Wlk. DE12: Mea 3G **37**
Norton Rd. DE13: Bur T 1F **13**
Nothill Rd. DE65: Hilt 4K **5**
Nottingham Rd. LE65: Ash Z, Lou 2B **32**
LE67: Cole 1B **34**
Nottingham Rd. Ind. Est. LE65: Ash Z 2C **32**
Nursery Cl. DE11: Swad 2J **21**
Nursery Gdns. LE67: Coal 1F **41**

O

Oadby Ri. DE13: Bur T 1F **13**
Oak Cl. DE11: Cas G 2F **29**
DE12: Mea 5F **37**
LE67: Coal 2H **41**
Oak Cres. LE65: Ash Z 2C **32**
Oak Dr. DE65: Hilt 3J **5**
LE67: Ibs 7A **40**
Oakfield Rd. DE13: Alre 7C **24**
Oakham Dr. LE67: Coal 7K **35**
Oakham Gro. LE65: Ash Z 2K **31**
Oaklands Rd. DE65: Etw 1D **6**
Oakleigh Av. DE11: New 3G **21**
Oakleigh Ct. *LE65: Ash Z* 3A **32**
(off Derby Rd.)
Oakley Grange DE13: Bur T 3C **12**
Oak Rd. DE13: Bar N 7G **17**
Oaks Ct. DE65: W'ton 1J **11**
Oaks Ind. Est. LE67: Coal 1B **40**
Oak Sq. DE11: Chu G 6G **21**
Oaks Rd. DE65: W'ton 1J **11**
LE67: Whit 3H **35**
Oak St. DE11: Chu G 6H **21**
DE14: Bur T 6G **13**
OAKTHORPE 4D **36**
Oakthorpe Sports & Leisure Cen. 3E **36**
Oaktree Bus. Pk. DE11: Swad 5F **21**
Oak Tree Cl. DE12: Cot E 5J **27**
Oak Tree Rd. LE67: Hug 3C **40**
Oakwood Cl. DE65: Hatt 5B **4**
Occupation La. DE11: Wood 7A **22**
Occupation Rd. DE11: Alb V 2J **29**
Octagon Centre, The DE14: Bur T 5J **13**
Oddfellows Row DE12: Mea 5F **37**
Odeon Cinema
Swadlincote 5K **21**
Old Bakery Cl. LE67: Thri 1E **34**
Old Church Cl. LE67: Hug 4E **40**
Olders Valley DE11: Wood 4B **22**
Oldfield Dr. DE11: Swad 3K **21**

Oldfield La. DE65: Hilt 5A 6
Old Forge Cl. DE65: Egg 1B 10
Old Hall Dr. DE65: W'ton 1J 11
Old Hall Gdns. DE11: Chu G 6H 21
Oldicote La. DE15: Bret 4F 15
Old Nurseries, The LE67: Rav 2A 40
Old Parks La. LE65: Smis 6K 23
Old Rd. DE14: Bran 1D 18
Old School Cl. LE67: Ell 7E 40
    LE67: Coal 1E 40
Old Station Cl. DE65: Etw 1C 6
    LE67: Coal 1E 40
Old Toll Ga. DE11: Wood 5B 22
Opening Hole Way DE11: Swad 4A 22
Orchard, The DE65: Rep 3K 11
Orchard Cl. DE12: Wal T 7C 18
    DE65: Hilt 4J 5
    DE65: W'ton 7J 7
    LE67: Rav 7A 34
Orchard Gdns. LE67: Whit 4F 35
Orchard Pk. DE14: Bur T 5J 13
Orchards, The LE67: Thri 1E 34
Orchard St. DE11: New 2G 21
    DE14: Bur T 5J 13
    LE67: Ibs 7B 40
Orchard Way DE12: Mea 5F 37
Orchid Cl. DE15: Stap 7B 14
Ordish Ct. DE14: Bur T 5J 13
                                (not continuous)
Ordish St. DE14: Bur T 5H 13
Ordley Wlk. DE65: Hilt 4J 5
                                (off Welland Rd.)
Orwell Rd. DE65: Hilt 4K 5
Osborne Cl. DE13: Bur T 1G 13
Osborne St. DE15: Win 4B 14
Osbourne Gdns. DE15: Win 4B 14
                                (off Osborne St.)
Osprey Cl. DE15: Win 3E 14
Otter Cl. LE67: Ibs 6A 40
Otter St. DE65: Hilt 4J 5
Oundle Cl. LE65: Ash Z 1J 31
Outfield Rd. DE15: Stap 7A 14
Outram Dr. DE11: Swad 4A 22
OUTWOODS
    DE13 . . . . .1G 13
    LE67 . . . . .1K 33
Outwoods Cl. DE13: Bur T 1F 13
                                (off Lwr. Outwoods Rd.)
Outwoods La. DE13: Ans, Bur T 7B 8
    LE67: Cole 1K 33
Outwoods St. DE14: Bur T 2G 13
Oval, The LE67: Coal 3H 41
OVERLEY 5A 24
Overley La. DE13: Alre 5A 24
OVERSEAL 6H 29
Overseal Mnr. Stables DE12: Ove 6J 29
Oversetts Ct. DE11: New 2G 21
Oversetts Rd. DE11: New 3F 21
Overton Cl. LE67: Cole 2K 33
OWEN'S BANK 7A 4
Owen's Bank DE13: Tut 7A 4
Owen St. LE67: Coal 1D 40
Oxford St. DE11: Chu G 7H 21
    DE14: Bur T 6G 13
    LE67: Coal 1F 41
Oxley Rd. DE15: Win 4B 14
Oyster Cl. DE14: Bran 1G 19

P

PACKINGTON 7B 32
Packington Nook La.
    LE65: Ash Z 5K 31
Paddock, The DE15: Win 3C 14
Paddocks, The DE11: New 3G 21
    DE13: Ans 7B 8
Page Cl. LE67: Coal .3H 41
Paget Rd. LE67: Ibs .5B 40
Paget St. DE14: Bur T 5H 13
Paisley Wlk. DE11: Chu G 7F 21
Palissy Cl. DE11: Swad 4K 21
Palmer Cl. DE13: Bar N 6G 17
    DE14: Bran 7G 13
Panama Rd. DE13: Bur T 1H 13
Paradise Cl. DE12: Moi 5D 30
Pares Cl. LE67: Whit 4F 35
Paris Cl. LE65: Ash Z 2K 31
Park Cl. DE12: Lin 3D 28
    DE13: Bar N 7F 17
    LE65: Ash Z 5K 31
Park Ct. DE11: Swad 3K 21
Parkdale LE67: Ibs .7A 40
Parkers Cl. DE11: Blac 1E 30
    LE67: Ell 7E 40
Parker St. DE14: Bur T 2J 13
Park La. DE13: Tut 7A 4
    DE65: Fos 1A 4
Park M. DE14: Bur T 5H 13
Park Pale, The DE13: Tut 1B 8

Park Rd. DE11: Chu G 6K 21
    DE11: New 4D 20
    DE12: Moi 7B 30
    DE12: Ove 3H 29
    DE13: Alre 6D 24
    DE13: Bar N 6F 17
    DE15: Stan 4D 20
    LE65: Ash Z 2A 32
    LE67: Coal 1E 40
Park Rd. Mobile Home Pk. DE11: Cas G 3G 29
Park Row DE15: Bret 6J 15
Park St. DE11: New .2H 21
    DE14: Bur T 5H 13
                                (not continuous)
Park Vw. DE11: New 2G 21
    LE67: Whit 4F 35
Park Vw. Cl. DE13: Stre 6A 10
Park Way DE65: Etw 1D 6
Parkway DE14: Bur T 6E 12
Parliament St. DE11: New 2G 21
Parsons Cl. DE11: Chu G 7H 21
Parsonwood Hill LE67: Whit 3F 35
Parsonwood Paddock LE67: Whit 4G 35
Partridge Dr. DE11: Wood 5C 22
Pass Courtyard LE65: Ash Z 3A 32
                                (off Market St.)
Pastures, The DE11: New 3G 21
    DE65: Rep 4K 11
Pastures La. DE12: Oak 3E 36
Patch Cl. DE13: Bur T 1G 13
Patrick Cl. DE12: Lin 4E 28
Paulet School Dr. DE15: Stap 1A 20
Paulyn Way LE65: Ash Z 4J 31
Pavilion Gro. DE14: Bur T 2G 13
Peacroft Ct. DE65: Hilt 3J 5
Peacroft La. DE65: Hilt 3J 5
Pear Tree Av. DE11: New 1G 21
Pear Tree Cl. DE11: Hart 1D 22
Pear Tree Cl. DE65: Etw 1C 6
Pear Tree Dr. DE12: Lin 3D 28
Peel Pl. DE13: Bar N 6G 17
Peel St. DE14: Bur T 6H 13
Pegasus Way DE65: Hilt 3K 5
Pegg Ct. DE13: Bur T 2A 12
Pegg's Cl. DE12: Mea 5F 37
Peggs Grange LE67: Hug 4E 40
PEGGS GREEN .1B 34
Peldar Pl. LE67: Coal 2J 41
Penistone St. LE67: Ibs 6B 40
Penkridge Rd. DE11: Chu G 7J 21
Pennine Way DE11: Swad 5H 21
    LE65: Ash Z 4A 32
Pensgreave Rd. DE13: Bur T 1G 13
Pentland Rd. LE65: Ash Z 3C 32
Percy Wood Cl. DE65: Hilt 3H 5
Peregrine Cl. DE12: Mea 6F 37
    DE15: Win 4E 14
Perran Av. LE67: Whit 7H 35
Pershore Dr. DE14: Bran 7F 13
Perth Cl. DE15: Win .5D 14
Peterfield Rd. LE67: Whit 6H 35
Peterleas, The DE12: Don 1B 36
Peters Ct. DE65: Hatt 4C 4
Peters St. DE11: Alb V 7K 21
Phoenix Pk. LE67: Coal 6C 34
Pickering Dr. LE67: Ell 6D 40
Piddocks Rd. DE15: Stan 3C 20
                                (not continuous)
Pine Cl. DE14: Bran .7F 13
    DE65: Etw 1D 6
    LE65: Ash Z 2C 32
Pine Ct. DE12: Moi 3E 30
    LE67: Bar H 6K 41
Pine Gro. DE11: New 2G 21
Pines, The LE67: Whit 6H 35
Pine Wlk. DE11: Cas G 2F 29
Pinewood Rd. DE15: Stap 2A 20
Pinfold Cl. DE13: Tut .1B 8
    DE65: Rep 7K 11
Pinfold La. DE65: Rep 7K 11
Pingle Farm Rd. DE11: New 3G 21
Pintail Ct. DE12: Mea 6E 36
                                (off Wigeon Dr.)
Piper La. LE67: Rav .1A 40
Pipers Way DE14: Bur T 2G 13
Pipeworks DE11: Swad 5K 21
Pipit Cl. LE67: Bar H .6F 37
Pirelli Stadium 7K 9
Pisca La. LE67: Hea . . . . .7H 39 & 4A 38
PISTERN HILLS .2J 23
Pithiviers Cl. LE65: Ash Z 4K 31
Pitt La. LE67: Cole 3K 33
Plantagenet Way LE65: Ash Z 2C 32
Plover Av. DE11: Wood 5C 22
Plummer Rd. DE11: New 2G 21
Plumtree Cotts. DE12: Don 1B 36
Pollard Way LE67: Rav 7B 34
Pool St. DE11: Chu G 6A 22
Pool Works DE11: Wood 7A 22

Poplar Av. DE11: Mid 2J 21
    DE12: Moi 7B 30
Poplar Dr. DE12: Mea 4F 37
Poplars Rd. DE13: Bur T 7H 9
Poppy Cl. LE67: Coal 3H 41
Poppy Gdns. DE13: Alre 7D 24
Porter's La. DE65: Fin 3K 7
                                (not continuous)
Portland Av. DE14: Bran 1F 19
Portland St. DE65: Etw 1C 6
Portsmouth Cl. DE11: Chu G 6F 21
Portway Dr. DE13: Tut 1B 8
Portwood Ind. Est. DE11: Chu G 7H 21
Postern Rd. DE13: Tate 3A 12
Post Office Rd. DE13: Alre 6D 24
Potlocks, The DE65: W'ton 7K 7
Potters Cft. DE11: Swad 3H 21
Potters Way DE13: Bar N 7H 17
Prentice Cl. DE12: Moi 5D 30
Preston's La. LE67: Cole 3K 33
Prestop Dr. LE65: Ash Z 2J 31
Prestwood Pk. Dr. DE11: Mid 3K 21
Pretoria Rd. LE67: Ell, Ibs 6C 40
Price Cl. DE14: Bur T 3E 12
                                (not continuous)
Primrose Dr. DE14: Bran 7F 13
Primrose Mdw. DE11: Mid 1J 21
Princess Av. DE12: Lin 4D 28
Princess Cl. DE11: Wood 6C 22
Princess St. DE11: Cas G 1G 29
    DE14: Bur T 3H 13
Princess Way DE13: Stre 6K 9
    DE14: Stre 6K 9
Prince St. LE67: Coal 2E 40
Priorfields LE65: Ash Z 4B 32
                                (not continuous)
Prior Pk. LE65: Ash Z 4B 32
Prior Pk. Rd. LE65: Ash Z 3A 32
Priory, The DE65: Rep 4K 11
Priory Cl. DE11: New 2H 21
    DE13: Tut 1A 8
    LE67: Thri 1D 34
Priory Lands DE13: Stre 4K 9
Private Rd. LE67: Hug 3C 40
                                (not continuous)
Provident Ct. DE11: Wood 6C 22

Q

Queens Ct. DE14: Bran 7G 13
Queens Dr. DE11: Swad 2J 21
QUEENS HOSPITAL 1F 13
Queensland Cres. DE15: Win 5D 14
Queens Ri. DE13: Tut 7B 4
Queen's St. DE12: Mea 5F 37
Queen St. DE11: Chu G 7H 21
    DE14: Bur T 6H 13
    LE67: Coal 2E 40
Queensway Ho. DE12: Mea 5F 37
Queen Victoria Dr. DE11: Swad 3J 21
Quelch Cl. LE67: Hug 4E 40
Quorn Cl. DE15: Stap 6B 14
Quorn Cres. LE67: Coal 2J 41

R

Radhurst Ri. DE13: Bar N 6F 17
Radleigh Grange DE11: Wood 6D 22
Radley Cl. LE65: Ash Z 1K 31
Raglan Cl. DE13: Stre 6J 9
Railway Cotts. DE65: Egg 6C 6
Railway Side DE11: Chu G 7J 21
Railway Ter. DE12: Mea 6F 37
Rambler Cl. DE11: New 3H 21
Ramscliff Av. DE12: Don 2C 36
Randall Dr. DE11: Swad 4J 21
Rangemore Hill DE13: Ran 2E 16
Rangemore Hill Cotts. DE13: Ran 1D 16
Rangemore St. DE14: Bur T 4G 13
Range Rd. LE65: Ash Z 3B 32
Ratcliff Cl. LE65: Ash Z 3K 31
Ratcliffe Av. DE14: Bran 7G 13
Raven Cl. DE12: Mea 6E 36
Raven Rd. DE13: Yox 2B 16
Ravenslea LE67: Rav 2K 39
RAVENSTONE 2A 40
Ravenstone Cl. LE67: Rav 2K 39
Ravenstone Rd. LE67: Coal 7B 34
    LE67: Hea 7H 39
    LE67: Ibs . . . . .5A 40 & 7K 39
Ravens Way DE14: Bur T 3G 13
Ravenwood DE11: Swad 5K 21
Rawdon Rd. DE12: Moi 3B 30
Rawdon Side DE11: Swad 4A 22
Reading Av. DE11: Chu G 7G 21
Rectory La. DE12: Stre F 6A 36
Rectory M. DE65: Egg 2C 10

Redburrow La. LE65: Pac 2B 38
  LE67: Nor H 3B 38
Red Hill La. LE67: Swan, Thri 4C 34
Redhill La. DE13: Tut 1A 8
Redhill Lodge Rd. DE11: New 1H 21
Redlands Est. LE67: Ibs 5C 40
Redmoor Cl. DE15: Win 4C 14
Redwood Dr. DE15: Stap 7B 14
Reeve End DE13: Yox 1B 16
Reform Rd. LE67: Ibs 7B 40
Regan Rd. DE12: Moi 5D 30
Regency Way DE13: Stre 6J 9
Regent Ct. DE11: Chu G 6J 21
                      (off Regent St.)
Regents Pk. Rd. DE14: Bran 1F 19
Regent St. DE11: Chu G 7H 21
Regs Way LE67: Bar H 5J 41
Reliant Cl. DE11: Wood 7B 22
Rempstone Rd. LE67: Cole 2H 33
Rennes Cl. LE65: Ash Z 3K 31
Renshaw Dr. DE11: New 3G 21
REPTON 3K 11
Repton Cl. LE65: Ash Z 1K 31
Repton Rd. DE11: Hart 1B 22
  DE12: Mea 5C 36
  DE15: New S 6F 11
  DE65: W'ton 1H 11
Rescue Way LE65: Ash Z 4A 32
Reservoir Hill DE11: Alb V 2A 30
  DE12: Moi 2A 30
Reservoir Rd. DE14: Bur T 3E 12
Reservoir Way DE11: Wood 7B 22
Resolution Rd. LE65: Ash Z 2C 32
Resthaven DE11: Swad 3J 21
Reynold's Dr. LE67: Cole 2G 33
Rhodes Ho. DE15: Win 4D 14
Ribble Cl. DE65: Hilt 5J 5
Richmond Ct. DE65: Rep 7K 11
Richmond Ho. DE65: Hilt 4H 5
Richmond Rd. LE67: Don H, Ibs 5D 40
Richmond St. DE14: Bur T 3H 13
Ricknild St. DE14: Bran 7E 12
Ridge, The DE15: New S 1C 14
Ridge End Dr. DE13: Bur T 6F 9
Ridgeway Rd. DE15: Stap 2K 19
Ridgway Rd. LE65: Ash Z 4J 31
Rink Dr. DE11: Swad 5J 21
Risborrow Cl. DE65: Etw 1F 7
Rise, The DE11: New 3G 21
Riverbank, The DE65: W'ton 1J 11
Riverdale Cl. DE15: Win 2C 14
River Sence Way LE67: Hug 4E 40
Riverside DE12: Wal T 7B 18
Riverside Centre, The DE14: Bur T 4K 13
Riverside Ct. DE12: Mea 6D 36
Riverside Dr. DE14: Bran 2E 18
Riverside Gdns. DE14: Bur T 2A 14
Riverside Pk. DE14: Bur T 1A 14
Rivoli Dr. DE11: Wood 7B 22
Robian Way DE11: Swad 4H 21
Robin Hood Cotts. DE13: Tate 1K 17
Robin Hood Pl. DE11: Chu G 6K 21
Robin Rd. LE67: Coal 2G 41
Robinson Rd. DE11: New 2G 21
  LE67: Whit 4E 34
Rochdale Cres. LE67: Coal 1K 41
Rockcliffe Cl. DE11: Chu G 7J 21
Rockingham Cl. LE65: Ash Z 4B 32
Rockland Ri. LE67: Whit 3G 35
Rockleigh Gdns. LE65: Ash Z 3K 31
Rodney Cl. DE65: Hilt 3K 5
Roedean Cl. LE65: Ash Z 2K 31
Rogers Ct. DE65: Hatt 4C 4
Rolleston La. DE13: Tut 1C 8
ROLLESTON ON DOVE 3G 9
Rolleston Rd. DE13: Bur T 5G 9
Rolleston Trad. Est. DE14: Bur T 2J 13
Romans Cres. LE67: Coal 1K 41
Roman Way DE12: Moi 5B 30
Rookery, The DE11: Wood 6C 22
  LE67: Hea 7G 39
Rookery Cl. DE13: Yox 2B 16
Rope Walk, The DE14: Bur T 6H 13
Ropewalk, The DE12: Wal T 7C 18
Rose Av. DE13: Stre 4B 10
Rosebank Vw. DE12: Mea 5E 36
Rose Cott. Cl. DE14: Bur T 6H 13
Rose Cott. Gdns. DE14: Bur T 6J 13
Rosecroft Gdns. DE11: Swad 6K 21
Rosedale LE67: Whit 2F 35
Rosedene Vw. DE12: Ove 5K 29
Rose Hill DE11: Wood 5B 22
Roseleigh Cres. DE11: New 2G 21
Rosemary Cres. LE67: Whit 5H 35
Rosemount Rd. DE15: Bur T 5A 14
Rose Tree La. DE11: New 1G 21
Rose Valley DE11: New 3H 21
Rosewood Rd. DE15: Stap 2A 20
ROSLISTON 3H 27

Rosliston Forestry Cen. 1H 27
Rosliston Rd. DE12: Ros, Wal T 1C 26
  DE15: Drak 1H 27
  DE15: Stap 2K 19
Rosliston Rd. Sth. DE15: Stap 3K 19
Rossall Dr. LE65: Ash Z 2K 31
Rosslyn Rd. LE67: Whit 5G 35
Rotherwood Dr. LE65: Ash Z 2A 32
Rothwell Ho. DE65: Hilt 4J 5
                      (off Otter St.)
Rouen Way LE65: Ash Z 2K 31
ROUGH HAY 3A 12
Rowan Av. LE67: Coal 2J 41
Rowan Cl. DE12: Mea 5F 37
  DE12: Moi 3E 30
Rowan Dr. LE67: Ibs 7A 40
Rowbury Dr. DE15: Bur T 5C 14
Rowena Dr. LE65: Ash Z 2A 32
Rowlands, The LE67: Cole 4K 33
Rowley Cl. DE11: Swad 3A 22
Rowley Ct. DE11: Swad 4J 21
Rowton St. DE13: Bur T 7G 9
Royal La. DE12: Ove 5J 29
Royal M. LE65: Ash Z 4A 32
Royal Oak Cl. LE67: Ibs 7A 40
Rugby Cl. DE14: Bur T 7H 13
  LE65: Ash Z 1K 31
Rumsey Cl. LE67: Thri 1D 34
Rushby Rd. LE67: Ell 7F 41
Rushton Cl. DE13: Tut 7B 4
Ruskin Pl. DE14: Bur T 1J 13
Russell St. DE11: Swad 5K 21
  DE14: Bur T 5J 13
Russet Cl. DE65: Hatt 4B 4
Ruston Cl. DE11: Swad 4J 21
Rutland Cl. DE15: Stap 2J 19
Rydal Gdns. LE65: Ash Z 5B 32
Ryder Cl. DE11: Swad 5F 21
Ryeflatts La. DE65: Hatt 4C 4
Rykneld Cl. DE14: Bran 1D 18
Rykneld St. DE13: Alre 7D 24
Ryknild Ind. Est. DE14: Bur T 1K 13
Ryton Way DE65: Hilt 5J 5

S

Saddlers Ct. DE12: Mea 5F 37
Saffron Cl. DE13: Bar N 7F 17
Sage Dr. DE11: Wood 4C 22
St Aidan's Cl. DE13: Bur T 7H 9
St Albans Ct. DE13: Bur T 7H 9
St Andrews Ct. DE11: Chu G 6F 21
St Andrew's Cl. LE67: Thri 1E 34
St Andrew's Dr. DE13: Bur T 6H 9
St Bernard's Rd. LE67: Whit 5G 35
St Catherine's Rd. DE11: New 3G 21
St Chad's Cl. DE13: Bur T 6H 9
St Chad's Rd. DE13: Bur T 6H 9
St Charles Cft. DE12: Mea 5G 37
St Christophers Pk. LE67: Ell 7F 41
St Christopher's Rd. LE67: Ell 7F 41
St Clares Ct. LE67: Coal 2F 41
St David's Ct. LE67: Coal 1K 41
St David's Cres. LE67: Coal 7K 35
St David's Dr. DE13: Bur T 6H 9
St Denys' Cres. LE67: Ibs 7A 40
St Edwards Ct. DE11: New 3G 21
St Faiths Dr. LE67: Coal 3D 40
St Francis Ct. DE13: Bur T 6J 9
St George's Hill LE67: Swan 2B 34
St Georges Rd. DE13: Bur T 2E 12
St Ives LE67: Coal 2J 41
St James Cl. DE11: Swad 3J 21
  DE65: W'ton 1K 11
St James Ct. DE13: Bar N 6G 17
St James' Rd. DE13: Bar N 7G 17
St John's Cl. LE67: Hea 7G 39
  LE67: Hug 4E 40
St John's Ct. DE13: Bur T 7H 9
St John's Dr. DE11: New 3F 21
St John's Rd. DE13: Bur T 7H 9
St Jude's Way DE13: Bur T 6H 9
St Luke's Rd. DE13: Bar N 7G 17
  DE13: Bur T 6H 9
St Margarets DE13: Bur T 2E 12
St Marks Rd. DE13: Bur T 6H 9
St Martins Cl. DE11: Chu G 7G 21
  DE13: Bur T 6G 9
St Mary's Av. LE67: Don H 4C 40
St Mary's Cl. DE15: New S 6F 11
St Mary's Ct. LE67: Don H 4C 40
St Mary's Dr. DE13: Stre 4A 10
                      (Dovecliff Cres.)
  DE13: Stre 6H 9
                      (St Luke's Rd.)
St Mary's La. LE67: Rav 3A 40
St Matthew's St. DE14: Bur T 1H 19

St Michael's Cl. DE65: W'ton 1J 11
  LE65: Ash Z 4B 32
St Michaels Dr. LE67: Rav 2K 39
St Michaels Rd. DE13: Bur T 6J 9
St Modwen Cl. DE13: Bur T 7H 9
St Modwen's Wlk. DE14: Bur T 5J 13
St Patricks Rd. DE13: Bur T 6H 9
St Paul's Cl. DE14: Bur T 4G 13
St Paul's Sq. DE14: Bur T 3G 13
St Paul's St. W. DE14: Bur T 3G 13
St Peter's Bri. DE14: Bur T 6J 13
  DE15: Bur T 6J 13
St Peters Cl. DE13: Hart 2E 22
St Peter's Ct. DE15: Stap 6A 14
St Peters Retail Pk. DE14: Bur T 6J 13
St Peter's St. DE15: Stap 6A 14
St Saviours Rd. LE67: Coal 2D 40
St Stephens Ct. DE11: Wood 5C 22
  DE13: Bur T 7H 9
St Vincents Cl. LE67: Coal 3D 40
Sales La. DE15: Win 4D 14
Salford Way DE11: Chu G 6F 21
Salisbury Av. DE15: Win 4D 14
Salisbury Dr. DE11: Mid 2B 22
Saltersford Valley Local Nature Reserve 3D 36
Salters Grn. Way DE13: Alre 6E 24
Salt Wlk. DE14: Bur T 5J 13
Samson Rd. LE67: Coal 6E 34
Sandalwood Rd. DE15: Stap 2K 19
Sandcliffe Pk. DE11: Mid 1A 22
Sandcliffe Rd. DE11: Mid 2A 22
Sandcroft Cl. DE11: Mid 3A 22
Sandford Brook DE65: Hilt 4K 5
Sandhills Cl. DE12: Mea 6F 37
Sandhole La. LE12: Shep 1K 35
Sandiway DE13: Bar N 1H 25
Sandlands, The DE11: Mid 2A 22
Sandown Cl. DE14: Bran 1F 19
Sandpits La. DE13: Yox 1A 16
Sandringham Av. DE15: Stap 6B 14
Sandringham Cl. DE11: Swad 3J 21
Sandringham Rd. LE67: Coal 2G 41
Sandtop Cl. DE11: Blac 1E 30
Sandtop La. DE11: Blac 1E 30
Sandy La. DE12: Cald 2A 28
Sandypits La. DE65: Etw 1D 6
Sankey Dr. DE11: Alb V 7K 21
Savey La. DE13: Yox 2A 16
Sawbridge Cl. LE67: Ell 7F 41
Saw Mill Way DE14: Bur T 3G 13
Sawpit La. DE65: Fos 3B 4
Saxon Cl. DE15: Stap 1A 20
Saxon Cft. DE65: Rep 6K 11
Saxon Gro. DE65: W'ton 1H 11
Saxon St. DE15: Stap 1A 20
Saxon Way LE65: Ash Z 2K 31
Scalpcliffe Cl. DE15: Bur T 5A 14
Scalpcliffe Rd. DE15: Bur T 4A 14
School Cl. DE11: Alb V 7K 21
School Grn. DE13: Yox 1A 16
School Ho. DE65: Rep 3K 11
School La. DE13: Rol D 2G 9
  LE67: Cole 1B 34
  LE67: Nor H 4E 38
  LE67: Whit 3E 34
School M. DE65: Hatt 4C 4
School St. DE11: Chu G 6J 21
  DE12: Moi 7C 30
  DE12: Oak 3D 36
School Yd. DE13: Bur T 1H 13
                      (off Rowton St.)
Scotch Hills La. DE13: Bar N 2C 16
Scotlands Dr. LE67: Coal 2E 40
Scotlands Ind. Est. LE67: Coal 2F 41
Scotlands Rd. LE67: Coal 2E 40
Scott Cl. LE65: Ash Z 2K 31
Scotts, The DE11: Cas G 1E 28
Scropton Old Rd. DE65: Hatt 5B 4
Scropton Rd. DE65: Hatt, Scro 4A 4
Seagrave Cl. LE67: Coal 1K 41
Sealey Cl. DE65: W'ton 1K 11
Seals Rd. DE12: Don 1B 36
Seal Vw. DE12: Lin 3D 28
Sealwood La. DE12: Lin, Ove 4E 28
                      (not continuous)
Second Av. DE14: Bur T 7D 12
Sedgefield Rd. DE14: Bran 1E 18
Sefton Cl. DE15: Stap 6C 14
Selina Cl. LE65: Ash Z 3B 32
Selwyn Cl. DE13: Alre 6D 24
Sence Valley Forest Pk. 5A 40
Seventh Av. DE14: Bur T 6E 12
Severn Cl. DE13: Stre 5H 9
Severn Dr. DE14: Bur T 4K 13
  DE65: Hilt 5J 5
Seymour Av. DE14: Bur T 7K 9
Shackland Dr. DE12: Mea 5G 37
Shady Gro. DE65: Hilt 3H 5
Shaef Cl. DE65: Hilt 3K 5

Shakespeare Cl.—Tellis Pl.

Shakespeare Cl. DE11: Swad 2K 21
Shakespeare Mdws. DE65: Rep 7K 11
Shakespeare Rd. DE14: Bur T 1H 13
Shannon App. DE14: Bur T 5J 13
Sharpe's Pottery Cen. 4J 21
Sharpley Av. LE67: Coal 7H 35
Sharpswood Mnr. DE11: Wood 4B 22
Sheffield St. DE14: Bur T 6H 13
SHELLBROOK 3H 31
Shellbrook Cl. LE65: Ash Z 3H 31
Shelley Av. DE14: Bur T 1J 13
Shelley Cl. DE12: Mea 7F 37
DE14: Bur T 1J 13
Shelley Rd. DE11: Swad 3K 21
Sherbourne Dr. DE14: Bran 1F 19
DE65: Hilt 4H 5
LE65: Ash Z 2K 31
Sherman Cl. DE65: Hilt 3K 5
Sherwood Cl. LE67: Ell 6E 40
Shie'ling, The DE65: Hatt 3B 4
Shiloh Cl. DE11: Wood 5B 22
Shipley Cl. DE14: Bran 7G 13
SHOBNALL 4F 13
Shobnall Cl. DE14: Bur T 3G 13
Shobnall Ct. DE14: Bur T 4G 13
Shobnall Leisure Complex 3F 13
Shobnall Rd. DE14: Bur T 4D 12
Shobnall St. DE14: Bur T 4G 13
SHORT HEATH 6A 30
Shortheath DE12: Sho H 6K 29
Shortheath Rd. DE12: Moi 6A 30
Short La. DE13: Bar N 7G 17
Short St. DE15: Stap 1K 19
Shotwood Cl. DE13: Rol D 2F 9
Shotwoodhill La. DE13: Rol D 1E 8
Shrewsbury Rd. DE13: Stre 4A 10
Shrewsbury Wlk. LE67: Thri 1E 34
Shrubbery, The DE11: Wood 6D 22
Sich La. DE13: Yox 4A 16
Siddalls St. DE15: Win 4C 14
Sidings Ind. Est. DE14: Bur T 3K 13
Silk Mill La. DE13: Tut 7B 4
Silkstone Cl. DE11: Chu G 7J 21
Silverhill Cl. DE13: Stre 5H 9
Silver St. DE12: Oak 4D 36
LE67: Whit 5F 35
Sinai Cl. DE14: Bur T 3E 12
Sinai Pk. DE13: Bur T 4D 12
SINOPE 6J 33
Sir Herbert Wragg Way DE11: Swad 5K 21
Siskin Cl. DE12: Mea 6E 36
Sixth Av. DE14: Bur T 5F 13
Skinner's La. LE67: Whit 4G 35
Skinners Way DE11: Mid, Swad 3A 22
Skylark Cl. DE12: Mea 6E 36
Skylark Way DE11: Swad 5A 22
Skyline Ct. DE14: Bur T 6E 12
Slackey La. DE12: Moi 5K 29
Slack La. DE11: Hart 2E 22
Slade Cl. DE65: Etw 1D 6
Slaybarns Way LE67: Ibs 6B 40
Small Mdws. La. DE13: Bar N 6H 17
Small Thorn Pl. DE11: Wood 6C 22
Smedley Cl. LE65: Ash Z 4J 31
Smedley Ct. DE65: Egg 1C 10
SMISBY 5J 23
Smisby Rd. LE65: Ash Z 6K 23
Smith Ct. LE67: Whit 4E 34
Smith Cres. LE67: Coal 1K 41
Smithy La. LE65: Ash Z 2D 32
SNIBSTON 3B 40
Snibston 1C 40
Snibston Country Pk. 1C 40
Snibston Ct. LE67: Coal 7C 34
Snibston Dr. LE67: Coal 7B 34
Snipe Cl. LE67: Hug 3C 40
Soar Cl. DE65: Hilt 4J 5
Solent Rd. DE11: Chu G 7F 21
Solney Cl. DE11: Swad 5G 21
Somerset Rd. DE15: Stap 2J 19
Somerville Rd. DE13: Alre 7C 24
Sorrel Dr. DE11: Wood 4B 22
Sth. Broadway St. DE14: Bur T 7H 13
South Cl. DE11: Blac 1E 30
South Dr. DE11: New 2G 21
Southgate Dr. DE15: Stap 5C 14
South Hill DE13: Rol D 2J 9
South La. LE67: Bar H 6K 41
Sth. Leicester Ind. Est. LE67: Ell 6F 41
Sth. Lodge M. DE11: Mid 3B 22
Sth. Oak St. DE14: Bur T 7G 13
South Rd. LE67: Ibs 7B 40
South St. DE11: Wood 7C 22
LE65: Ash Z 3A 32
LE67: Ell 6E 40
Sth. Uxbridge St. DE14: Bur T 7G 13
Sovereign Bus. Pk. DE14: Bur T 2K 13
Sovereign Dr. DE14: Bran 7G 13
Sparkenhoe Est. LE67: Hea 7G 39
Speedwell Cl. DE11: Wood 4C 22
LE67: Coal 1F 41
Spencer Cl. DE13: Stre 5J 9
Spencer Vw. LE67: Ell 7F 41
Sperry Ct. LE67: Ibs 7B 40
Spilsbury Cl. DE65: W'ton 1J 11
Spinney, The LE67: Hug 4D 40
Spinney Cl. LE65: Ash Z 4A 32
Spinney Lodge DE65: Rep 4K 11
Spinney Rd. DE14: Bran 7E 12
Spode Dr. DE11: Wood 7C 22
Spring Cl. DE11: Cas G 7G 21
Spring Cott. Rd. DE12: Ove 5K 29
Spring Farm Rd. DE15: Stap 6B 14
Springfield LE67: Thri 1F 35
Springfield Cl. DE11: Mid 2J 21
LE67: Ibs 7B 40
Springfield Rd. DE11: Mid, Swad 3J 21
DE65: Etw 2C 6
DE65: Rep 7K 11
Springfield Vs. *DE15: Stap* *6B 14*
(off Grafton Rd.)
Springhill DE11: Hart 1D 22
Springhill Cotts. DE11: Hart 1D 22
Spring La. LE65: Pac 7B 32
LE67: Coal, Swan 5C 34
Spring Mdws. LE67: Swan 5C 34
Spring Rd. LE67: Ibs 6C 40
Spring St. DE11: Cas G 1H 29
Spring Ter. Rd. DE15: Stap 6A 14
Springwood Farm Rd. DE11: Mid 1J 21
Square, The DE12: Oak 3D 36
DE13: Rol D *2F 9*
(off Mosley M.)
DE15: Bret 4J 15
Squirrel Wlk. DE12: Ove 6J 29
Stable M. DE11: Wood 6C 22
Stadium Cl. LE67: Coal 2D 40
Stafford St. DE14: Bur T 2J 13
Stainsdale Grn. LE67: Whit 7H 35
Staley Av. LE65: Ash Z 5J 31
Staley Cl. DE11: Swad 6J 21
Stamford Dr. LE67: Coal 7K 35
Stamps Cl. DE15: Win 4D 14
Standard Hill LE67: Hug 3C 40
Standing Butts Cl. DE12: Wal T 1C 26
STANHOPE BRETBY 6F 15
Stanhope Glade DE15: Bret 7H 15
Stanhope Grn. DE15: Bret 6G 15
Stanhope Rd. DE11: Swad 5J 21
Stanhope St. DE15: Win 4C 14
Stanleigh Gdns. DE12: Don 2B 36
Stanleigh Rd. DE12: Ove 5J 29
Stanley Cl. DE11: Wood 5C 22
Stanley St. DE11: Swad 4K 21
DE14: Bur T 5H 13
STANTON 3C 20
Stanton Rd. DE15: Stan, Stap 7A 14
STAPENHILL 6A 14
Stapenhill Rd. DE15: Bur T, Stap 6A 14
Staples Dr. LE67: Coal 2J 41
Statfold La. DE13: Alre 5C 24
Station Ct. DE14: Bur T 4H 13
Station Dr. DE12: Moi 5C 30
Station Hill LE67: Swan 5B 34
Station La. DE12: Wal T 7B 18
Station M. LE65: Ash Z 4A 32
Station Rd. DE11: Wood 6C 22
DE13: Bar N 7G 17
DE13: Rol D 2G 9
DE65: Fos, Hatt 5B 4
LE65: Ash Z 4A 32
LE67: Hug 5D 40
LE67: Ibs 7A 40
Station St. DE11: Cas G 1G 29
DE14: Bur T 4H 13
Station St. Bus. Cen. *DE14: Bur T* *4H 13*
(off Station St.)
Station Wlk. DE13: Stre 5K 9
Station Yd. DE13: Alre 7E 24
Stenson Rd. LE67: Coal 7E 34
Stephenson Ct. LE67: Coal 7B 34
Stephenson Ind. Est. LE67: Coal 7C 34
Stephenson Way LE67: Coal 6B 34
Stephens Rd. DE14: Bran 7G 13
Stewart Cl. DE14: Bran 2F 19
Stimpson Rd. LE67: Coal 1F 41
Stinson Way LE67: Whit 4E 34
Stirling Cl. DE11: Chu G 7G 21
Stirling Ri. DE13: Stre 6J 9
Stockton Cl. DE11: Chu G 6G 21
Stonebridge Cl. LE67: Ibs 6A 40
Stonehaven Cl. LE67: Coal 1K 41
Stone Row LE67: Coal 7E 34
Stoneydale Cl. DE11: New 3G 21
Stoney La. LE67: Cole 2K 33
Stour Cl. DE65: Hilt 5K 5
Stowe Cl. LE65: Ash Z 2K 31
Stranger's La. DE13: Yox 6A 16
Stratford Cl. DE65: Rep 7K 11
Strathmore Cl. LE67: Coal 2K 41
Strawberry La. DE11: Blac 1E 30
DE12: Ros 4J 27
STRETTON 5K 9
Stretton Dr. LE67: Coal 1K 41
STRETTON EN LE FIELD 6A 36
Stretton Vw. DE12: Oak 4C 36
Stuart Way LE65: Ash Z 4A 32
Sudbury Rd. DE13: Yox 1B 16
Suffolk Rd. DE15: Stap 2J 19
Suffolk Way DE11: Chu G 7F 21
Summerfields Dr. DE11: Mid 2A 22
Sunningdale Cl. DE13: Stre 5H 9
Sunningdale Rd. LE67: Coal 2G 41
Sunnyside DE11: New 1F 21
LE67: Ibs 7A 40
Sunnyside Ct. DE11: New 1G 21
Sun St. DE11: Wood 6C 22
Sussex Rd. DE15: Stap 2J 19
Sutton La. DE65: Etw 1C 6
DE65: Fos, Hilt 3D 4
DE65: Hilt 1G 5
Sutton Pl. DE11: Wood 6C 22
Suttons Av. DE11: Wood 7B 22
Suttons Bus. Pk. DE11: Wood 5B 22
SWADLINCOTE 5J 21
Swadlincote La. DE11: Chu G 7E 20
(not continuous)
Swadlincote Rd. DE11: Wood 5A 22
Swadlincote Ski & Snowboard Cen. 5K 21
Swadlincote Woodlands Forest Pk. 4A 22
Swainsfield Rd. DE13: Yox 2B 16
SWAINSPARK 2J 29
Swainspark Ind. Est. DE12: Ove 2J 29
Swainswood DE11: Cas G, Chu G 2J 29
Swallow Cl. DE13: Alre 6D 24
Swallow Dale LE67: Thri 2E 34
Swallow Rd. DE11: Wood 5C 22
Swan Ct. DE15: Bur T 4A 14
Swannington Incline LE67: Swan 4C 34
SWANNINGTON 4B 34
Swannington Rd. LE67: Coal 1A 40
Swannington St. DE13: Bur T 1G 13
Swannington Windmill 2B 34
Swannymote Rd. LE67: Whit 3H 35
Swans Rest DE11: New 2G 21
Swan Wlk. DE14: Bur T 5J 13
Swan Way LE67: Coal 2G 41
Swarbourn Cl. DE13: Yox 2B 16
Sweethill DE12: Moi 4D 30
SWEPSTONE 7C 38
Swepstone Rd. DE12: Mea 5H 37
LE67: Hea, Swep 7D 38
Swift Cl. DE11: Wood 5C 22
Swifts Cl. LE67: Ibs 6B 40
Swinfen Cl. LE67: Ell 7D 40
Swithland Rd. LE67: Coal 2K 41
Sycamore Av. DE11: New 1H 21
Sycamore Cl. DE12: Lin 4E 28
DE15: Stap 3K 19
DE65: Etw 1D 6
LE67: Ibs 7A 40
Sycamore Ct. DE15: Stan 2A 20
DE65: W'ton 1J 11
Sycamore Dr. DE12: Moi 3E 30
LE65: Ash Z 2C 32
Sycamore Rd. DE15: Stap 3K 19
LE67: Coal 2H 41
Sycamores, The DE11: Wood 4B 22
DE13: Tut 7C 4
Sydney St. DE14: Bur T 1J 13

T

Tailby Dr. DE65: W'ton 1H 11
Talbot La. LE67: Swan, Thri, Whit 2C 34
Talbot Pl. DE12: Don 2B 36
Talbot St. DE11: Chu G 6H 21
LE67: Whit 2E 34
Tamworth Rd. DE12: App M, Mea 7B 36
LE65: Ash Z 5K 31
Tandy Av. DE12: Moi 4E 30
Tanner's La. DE65: Rep 3J 11
Tan Yd. LE67: Swan 4C 34
Tapton Pk. Ind. Est. DE11: Wood 7B 22
Tara St. LE67: Bar H 6J 41
Tarquin Cl. DE13: Stre 4K 9
TATENHILL 7A 12
Tatenhill La. DE14: Bran 1C 18
Tavistock Cl. LE67: Hug 4D 40
Tayleur Cl. LE67: Coal 2F 41
Taylor Cl. DE12: Moi 5D 30
Teal Cl. LE67: Coal 2G 41
Tean Cl. DE15: Stap 6B 14
Teasel Dr. DE11: Wood 4C 22
Telford Way LE67: Coal 6B 34
Tellis Pl. DE12: Mea 5G 37

Telmah Cl. DE13: Stre 5J 9
Templars Way LE67: Whit 4G 35
Temple Cl. DE14: Bur T 7J 9
Temple Hill LE67: Whit 3G 35
Tennyson Av. DE11: Swad 2K 21
Tennyson Cl. DE12: Mea 6E 36
Tennyson Rd. DE14: Bur T 7J 9
Tern Av. DE11: Wood 5C 22
TETRON POINT 5E 20
Tetron Point Golf Course 4F 21
Thames Way DE65: Hilt 4J 5
The . . . .
   Names prefixed with 'The' for example
   'The Abbey' are indexed under the main
   name such as 'Abbey, The'

Third Av. DE14: Bur T 6E 12
Thirlmere LE67: Coal 1K 41
Thirlmere Gdns. LE65: Ash Z 5B 32
Thistle Cl. DE11: Wood 4C 22
Thomas Ct. LE67: Coal 1D 40
Thomas Rd. LE67: Whit 4E 34
Thomas St. LE67: Ibs 7B 40
Thompson Cl. DE11: Wood 4B 22
THORNBOROUGH 6D 34
Thornborough Rd. LE67: Coal 7D 34
Thorndale LE67: Ibs 7A 40
Thornescroft Gdns. DE14: Bran 1G 19
Thornewill Dr. DE13: Stre 5A 10
Thornham Gro. LE67: Ibs 6B 40
Thornhill Cl. DE13: Bar N 6F 17
Thornley St. DE14: Bur T 1H 13
Thorn St. DE11: Wood 6C 22
Thorn St. M. DE11: Wood 6C 22
Thornton Cl. LE67: Coal 1K 41
Thorntop Cl. DE11: Blac 1E 30
Thorntree Cl. LE67: Rav 7A 34
Thorn Tree La. DE15: Bret 7G 15
Thorntree La. DE11: New 1G 21
Thorpe Cl. DE15: Stap 6D 14
Thorpe Downs Rd. DE11: Chu G 7J 21
Thrift Rd. DE14: Bran 7G 13
THRINGSTONE 2E 34
Thrushton Cl. DE65: Fin 4K 7
Ticknall Rd. DE11: Hart 1E 22
Tideswell Grn. DE11: New 3F 21
Tiger Ct. DE14: Bur T 5H 13
Tilley Grn. DE11: New 2G 21
Tinsell Brook DE65: Hilt 4J 5
Tintagel Cl. DE13: Stre 4K 9
Tithe Cl. LE67: Thri 1D 34
Tiverton Av. LE67: Whit 7H 35
Tom Bill Way LE65: Ash Z 7K 23
Tooth St. DE11: Wood 7B 22
Topmeadow DE11: Mid 1J 21
Torrance Cl. DE14: Bran 2F 19
Torrington Av. LE67: Whit 7H 35
Totnes Cl. DE13: Stre 7J 9
   LE67: Hug .4D 40
Toulmin Dr. DE11: Swad 4J 21
Toulouse Pl. LE65: Ash Z 3K 31
Tourist Info. Cen.
   Ashby-de-la-Zouch 3A 32
   Burton upon Trent 5K 13
   Swadlincote 4J 21
Tournament Way LE65: Ash Z 1K 31
Tower Gdns. LE65: Ash Z 3K 31
Tower Rd. DE11: Hart 2D 22
   DE15: Bur T 5C 14
Town Hill DE13: Yox 2B 16
Townsend La. LE67: Don H 5C 40
Toys of Yesteryear Mus. 7J 17
Tramway, The DE11: New 1G 21
Trent Av. DE65: W'ton 1J 11
Trent Bri. DE14: Bur T 4K 13
   LE67: Coal .3H 41
Trent Cl. DE65: W'ton 1K 11
Trentham Cl. *LE65: Ash Z* 3A 32
              (off North St.)
Trent Ind. Est. DE14: Bur T 3K 13
Trent La. DE15: New S 6F 11
Trent St. DE14: Bur T 6H 13
Trent Ter. *DE14: Bur T* 4K 13
              (off Bridge St.)
Trent Vw. *DE15: Stap* 1J 19
            (off Waterside Rd.)
Trent Washlands 5K 13
Tressall Rd. LE67: Whit 6H 35
Trevelyan Cl. DE15: Stap 5D 14
Trinity Cl. LE65: Ash Z 3K 31
Trinity Ct. LE65: Ash Z 3A 32
Trinity Gro. DE11: Swad 5J 21
Trinity Sq. DE14: Bur T 4J 13
Tristram Gro. DE13: Stre 4K 9
Troon Cl. DE13: Stre 5H 9
Truro Cl. DE11: Mid 3B 22
Trusley Brook DE65: Hilt 4J 5
Trusley Cl. DE14: Bran 1G 19
Tudor Cl. LE65: Ash Z 4A 32
Tudor Ct. DE13: Tut 7A 4

Tudor Hollow DE13: Stre 6J 9
Tudor Ho. Cl. DE11: New 1H 21
Tudor Way DE11: New 2H 21
Tunicliffe Cl. DE11: Swad 4A 22
Turnbury Cl. DE14: Bran 1F 19
Turolough Rd. LE67: Whit 2F 35
Turton Cl. DE13: Alre 7D 24
TUTBURY 7B 4
Tutbury & Hatton Station (Rail) 5C 4
Tutbury Castle 6A 4
Tutbury Cl. LE65: Ash Z 4B 32
Tutbury Crystal 7B 4
Tutbury Mus. .7B 4
Tutbury Rd. DE13: Bur T, Tut 4E 8
Tutbury Rd. Rural DE13: Bur T 4E 8
Twayblade DE14: Bran 7G 13
Tweentown LE67: Don H 5D 40
Twentylands DE13: Rol D 2J 9
Twyford Cl. DE11: Swad 6G 21
   DE65: W'ton 1K 11
   LE67: Coal .1K 41
Twyford Rd. DE65: W'ton 7J 7
Tynefield Ct. DE65: Etw 3C 6
Tynefield M. DE65: Etw 3B 6
Tythe, The DE13: Mid 1J 21

U

Uldale Gro. DE11: Chu G 7K 21
Ulleswater Cres. LE65: Ash Z 5B 32
Underhill Wlk. DE14: Bur T 5J 13
Union Pas. LE65: Ash Z 3A 32
Union Rd. DE11: Swad 3J 21
Union St. DE14: Bur T 5J 13
Unity Cl. DE11: Chu G 7H 21
Uplands Rd. DE12: Mea 6F 37
Up. Church St. LE65: Ash Z 3B 32
UPPER MIDWAY 1J 21
UPPER OUTWOODS 6D 8
Up. Packington Rd. LE65: Ash Z 5B 32
Uppingham Dr. LE65: Ash Z 2K 31
Usbourne Way LE67: Ibs 6A 40
Utah Cl. DE65: Hilt 3K 5
Uttoxeter Rd. DE65: Fos 2A 4
Uxbridge St. DE14: Bur T 6H 13

V

Vale Rd. DE11: Hart 5D 22
   DE11: Mid .2J 21
Valley Ri. DE11: Swad 3H 21
Valley Rd. DE12: Ove 6H 29
   LE67: Ibs 7A 40
Valley Way LE67: Whit 4E 34
Vancouver Dr. DE15: Win 4D 14
Vaughan St. LE67: Coal 2D 40
Venture Theatre, The 3A 32
Vercor Cl. *LE67: Coal* 1K 41
           (off Romans Cres.)
Verdon Cres. LE67: Coal 1J 41
Vere Cl. DE65: W'ton 1J 11
Vernon Ter. DE14: Bur T 3H 13
Via Devana DE12: Moi 6B 30
Vicarage Cl. DE11: Blac 1F 31
   DE15: Win .3C 14
Vicarage Fld. *DE15: Stap* 6A 14
           (off St Peter's Ct.)
Vicarage Gdns. DE11: Swad 4K 21
Vicarage La. LE65: Pac 7A 32
Vicarage Rd. DE11: Swad 4K 21
   DE11: Wood 6B 22
Vicarage St. LE67: Whit 4G 35
Vicarage Wlk. DE12: Ros 3H 27
Victoria Cl. LE67: Whit 4E 34
Victoria Ct. DE12: Ove 5H 29
Victoria Cres. DE14: Bur T 2H 13
Victoria Dr. DE11: Wood 7B 22
Victoria Rd. DE14: Bur T 3H 13
   LE67: Coal .1E 40
   LE67: Ibs 5B 40
Victoria St. DE13: Yox 1B 16
   DE14: Bur T 3H 13
Victoria Vs. DE11: New 2H 21
Viking Bus. Cen. DE11: Wood 5C 22
Village M. DE14: Bur T 5H 13
Violet Cl. DE12: Don 1B 36
Violet La. DE15: Stap 7A 14
Violet Way DE15: Stap 7A 14
Vulcan Ct. LE67: Coal 7E 34
Vulcan Way LE67: Coal 7E 34

W

Waggon La. DE15: Bret 6G 15
Wainwright Rd. LE67: Hug 4E 40
Wakefield Av. DE13: Tut 7A 4

Wakefield Dr. LE67: Whit 4F 35
Wakelyn Cl. DE65: Hilt 3H 5
Wales La. DE13: Bar N 7G 17
Walford Rd. DE13: Rol D 2J 9
Walker Rd. LE67: Bar H 6K 41
Walker St. DE14: Bur T 6G 13
Walkfield Rd. DE13: Alre 7C 24
Wall Rd. DE14: Bran 7F 13
Walnut Cl. DE11: New 3H 21
Walton Cl. DE11: Swad 6H 21
Walton La. DE13: Bar N 7A 18
WALTON-ON-TRENT 7C 18
Walton Rd. DE15: Drak 5F 19
Walton Vs. DE13: Ans 7B 8
Warren Cl. DE13: Stre 5K 9
Warren Dr. DE12: Lin 3C 28
Warren Hill DE11: New 3F 21
Warren Hills Rd. LE67: Coal 6K 35
Warren La. DE14: Bran 1E 18
   LE67: Whit .2G 35
Warwick Cl. DE11: Mid 2B 22
   DE14: Bran 7E 12
Warwick St. DE14: Bur T 1H 13
Warwick Way LE65: Ash Z 4B 32
Washford Rd. DE65: Hilt 5A 5
Wash La. LE67: Rav 2A 40
Watchorn Cl. DE11: Swad 3A 22
Waterloo Pl. DE11: Swad 5J 21
Waterloo St. DE14: Bur T 4H 13
Water Mdw. Way LE67: Ibs 7B 40
Waterside DE15: Stap 7K 13
   DE65: W'ton 7H 7
Waterside Ct. DE14: Bur T 6E 12
Waterside Rd. DE15: Stap 2H 19
Waterton Cl. DE13: Stre 5B 10
Waterworks Rd. LE67: Coal 3H 41
Watery La. DE11: New 3E 20
   DE15: Bret 4J 15
Watson St. DE14: Bur T 5J 13
Waveney Ct. DE65: Hilt 3H 5
Waverley La. DE14: Bur T 4G 13
Weathernfield DE12: Lin 4E 28
Weaverlake Dr. DE13: Yox 1A 16
Weavers Cl. LE67: Whit 6F 35
WEAVERSLAKE 1B 16
Wedgewood Cl. DE15: Stap 3C 14
Wedgewood Way DE11: Wood 7C 22
Weir Bank DE15: Stap 2K 19
Welford Ri. DE13: Stre 7F 9
Welland Cl. DE15: Win 2B 14
   LE67: Coal .2H 41
Welland Rd. DE65: Hilt 4H 5
Wellfield Rd. DE13: Alre 7D 24
Wellington Ct. LE67: Ibs 6B 40
Wellington Pk. DE14: Bran 7F 13
Wellington Rd. DE14: Bur T 1D 18
Wellington St. DE14: Bur T 4G 13
Wellington St. E. DE14: Bur T 4G 13
Wellington St. W. DE14: Bur T 4G 13
Well La. DE14: Blac 7E 22
   DE65: Rep .5K 11
Wells Rd. LE65: Ash Z 5J 31
Wellwood Rd. DE11: New 2H 21
Wentworth Dr. DE13: Stre 5J 9
Wentworth Rd. LE67: Coal 2D 40
Wesley Hillman Ct. *DE12: Mea* 5F 37
            (off Pegg's Cl.)
Westacre Dr. DE11: Chu G 6G 21
West Av. DE65: Hilt 3H 5
Western Av. LE67: Coal 7B 34
Western Cl. LE65: Ash Z 5A 32
Western Pk. LE65: Ash Z 5K 31
Westfield Rd. DE11: Swad 3J 21
   DE13: Bur T 7G 9
Westfields Av. LE65: Ash Z 3J 31
Westfields Ter. LE65: Ash Z 2J 31
West La. LE67: Bar H, Ell 7J 41
West Lawn DE65: Fin 3K 7
Westmead Rd. DE13: Bar N 7F 17
Westminster Dr. DE11: Chu G 7F 21
   DE13: Stre .6J 9
Westminster Ind. Est. DE12: Mea 6E 36
Westminster Way LE65: Ash Z 1K 31
Weston Pk. Av. DE14: Bur T 7J 9
Weston St. DE11: Swad 5J 21
   DE15: Win .4C 14
West St. DE11: Swad 4J 21
Westwood Pk. DE11: New 3G 21
Wetherby Ct. DE14: Bran 1E 18
Wetherel Rd. DE15: Stap 5D 14
Wetlands Way DE11: Swad 4A 22
WETMORE 1A 14
Wetmore La. DE14: Bur T 1A 14
Wetmore Rd. DE14: Bur T 1K 13
Wetmore Rd. Ind. Est. *DE14: Bur T* 2K 13
            (off Wharf Rd.)
Wharf Rd. DE14: Bur T 2K 13
Wharf Rd. Ind. Est. DE14: Bur T 2K 13

Whatton Est. LE67: Cole 2G 33
Wheat Breach Cl. DE13: Bur T 1G 13
Wheatfield Ct. DE65: W'ton 1K 11
Wheatlands DE11: Mid 1J 21
Wheatlands Rd. DE15: Stap 1K 19
Wheatley La. DE15: Win 3C 14
Whetstone Dr. LE67: Coal 1F 41
Whinchat Ct. DE12: Mea 6E 36
(off Wigeon Dr.)
White Hart M. DE13: Alre 6D 24
White Heart M. DE13: Alre 5A 24
Whitehill Rd. LE67: Ell 7E 40
Whitehouse Way DE12: Newt 4F 37
White Leys Ct. LE67: Coal 1D 40
(off Melbourne St.)
Whitestone La. DE13: Ans 5B 8
WHITWICK 4G 35
Whitwick Bus. Pk. LE67: Coal 7E 34
(not continuous)
Whitwick Moor LE67: Thri 2E 34
Whitwick Rd. LE67: Coal 1E 40
Whitworth Cl. DE12: Moi 5B 30
Wickets, The DE15: Stap 7A 14
Wideshaft DE11: Swad 4K 21
Wigeon Dr. DE12: Mea 6E 36
Wildgoose Cl. LE67: Ibs 6B 40
Wildhay Brook DE65: Hilt 4H 5
Wilfred Gdns. LE65: Ash Z 4K 31
Wilfred Pl. LE65: Ash Z 4K 31
Wilkes Av. DE12: Mea 6F 37
Wilkins La. DE13: Alre 7C 24
Willars Way LE67: Rav 2A 40
Willcock Rd. DE14: Bran 1F 19
Willesley Cl. LE65: Ash Z 5J 31
Willesley Gdns. LE65: Ash Z 5J 31
Willesley La. LE65: W'ley 6H 31
Willesley Pk. Golf Course 5J 31
Willesley Rd. LE65: Ash Z, W'ley 7G 31
Willesley Woodside LE65: Ash Z, Pac, W'ley 4E 30
(not continuous)
William IV Rd. DE13: Alre 6D 24
William Bees Rd. LE67: Coal 2E 40
William Nadin Way DE11: Swad 5F 21
William Newton Cl. DE65: Egg 1C 10
William St. DE14: Bur T 2H 13
WILLINGTON 1H 11
Willington Gravel Pits Nature Reserve 2G 11
Willington Rd. DE65: Chu 1C 6
DE65: Fin 6K 7
DE65: Rep 2J 11
DE65: W'ton 7K 7
Willington Station (Rail) 1H 11
Willn Cl. LE67: Coal 2J 41
Willowbrook Cl. DE65: Hilt 3H 5
LE65: Ash Z .1A 32
Willowbrook Farm (Camping & Caravan Site)
DE13: Alre 5F 25
Willow Cl. DE12: Mea 4F 37
DE12: Moi 3E 30
Willow Ct. DE11: Swad 4K 21
Willow Dr. DE11: New 1G 21
Willowfields DE65: Hilt 3J 5

Willow Grn. LE67: Coal 7K 35
Willow Gro. DE65: W'ton 7H 7
Willow Pit La. DE65: Hilt 1K 5
Willow Pl. DE15: Stap 1K 19
Willow Rd. DE13: Bar N 7G 17
Willows, The DE14: Bur T 5J 13
(off Park St.)
Willowsend Cl. DE65: Fin 4K 7
Willow Way LE67: Ibs 7A 40
Wilmot Pas. DE11: Swad 5J 21
Wilmot Rd. DE11: Swad 5J 21
Winchcombe Dr. DE15: Stap 6C 14
Winchester Cl. LE67: Ibs 6B 40
Winchester Dr. DE11: Mid 2A 22
DE12: Lin 4E 28
DE14: Bur T .7H 13
Winchester Way LE65: Ash Z 2K 31
Windermere Av. LE65: Ash Z 4B 32
Windermere Dr. DE65: Hilt 4K 5
Windmill Cl. LE65: Ash Z 4B 32
LE67: Rav 3K 39
Windmill Rd. DE65: Etw 2C 6
Windmill St. DE11: Chu G 7H 21
Windmill Vw. LE67: Swan 3B 34
Windrush Rd. DE65: Hilt 5J 5
Windsor Cl. DE11: New 2H 21
LE67: Coal 1J 41
Windsor Dr. DE15: Stap 6A 14
Windsor Ind. Est.
DE14: Bur T .2K 13
Windsor Rd. DE12: Lin 4E 28
LE65: Ash Z .4A 32
WINSHILL 4C 14
Winster Grn. DE11: New 3F 21
Witham Cl. DE65: Hilt 3K 5
Wolfscote Dale DE11: Chu G 6G 21
Wolsey Rd. LE67: Coal 7D 34
Woodbine Cl. DE14: Bran 2D 18
Woodcock Way LE65: Ash Z 2B 32
Woodcote LE65: Ash Z 1A 32
Wood Ct. DE14: Bur T 6H 13
Wood Farm La. DE11: Wood 4B 22
Woodfield Cotts. DE12: Mea 5G 37
Woodfield Dr. DE11: Swad 3K 21
Woodhouse Rd. LE67: Coal 2J 41
Woodhouse St. DE11: Wood 5A 22
Woodland Rd. DE15: Stan 2B 20
Woodlands, The DE13: Tate 7A 12
Woodlands Cres. DE12: Ove 5H 29
Woodlands Rd. DE12: Ove 5J 29
Woodlands Way DE12: Moi 3E 30
Wood La. DE11: New 1G 21
Woodmans Cft. DE65: Hatt 4B 4
Woods Cl. DE15: Stap 6B 14
LE67: Hug 4D 40
Woodside LE65: Ash Z 4J 31
Woods La. DE15: Stap 7A 14
(not continuous)
Wood St. DE11: Chu G 6J 21
DE14: Bur T .6H 13
LE65: Ash Z .3B 32

Woodview Rd. DE11: New 3E 20
WOODVILLE 5C 22
Woodville Rd. DE11: Hart 4C 22
DE12: Ove 6J 29
Woodwards Pl. DE11: Swad 5K 21
Woodward Way DE11: Swad 4A 22
Woodyard Cl. DE11: Cas G 7G 21
Woolrooms, The LE67: Cole 1A 34
Woosnam Cl. DE14: Bran 2F 19
Worcester Rd. DE15: Stap 2K 19
Wordsworth Av. DE11: Swad 3K 21
Wordsworth Cl. DE14: Bur T 1J 13
LE67: Cole 2K 33
Wordsworth Way DE12: Mea 7E 36
Workspace 17 LE67: Coal 3D 40
Worthington Way
DE14: Bur T .5J 13
Wortley Cl. LE67: Coal 1F 41
Woulds Ct. DE12: Moi 3E 30
(off Sycamore Dr.)
Wrekin Cl. LE65: Ash Z 5B 32
Wren Cl. DE11: Wood 5C 22
Wren Pk. Cl. DE65: Fin 4K 7
Wyatt Rd. LE67: Coal 7F 35
WYCHNOR 4E 24
Wye Cl. DE65: Hilt .5J 5
Wye Dale DE11: Chu G 6G 21
Wyggeston Rd. LE67: Coal 2E 40
Wyggeston St.
DE13: Bur T .1G 13
Wylam Cl. LE67: Coal 6C 34
Wyllie M. DE14: Bur T 4J 13
Wyndham Cres. DE15: Win 4D 14
Wystan Ct. DE65: Rep 7K 11
Wyston Brook DE65: Hilt 4J 5

Y

Yard Cl. DE11: Swad 4J 21
Yarrow Cl. DE15: Stap 5C 14
Yates Cl. DE12: Moi 4D 30
Yew Tree Ct. DE65: Hatt 3B 4
Yew Tree Cres. DE15: Stap 1A 20
Yew Tree Gdns.
DE12: Ros 3H 27
Yew Tree Rd. DE11: New 1G 21
DE12: Ros 3H 27
DE65: Hatt 3C 4
York Cl. DE11: Mid 2A 22
DE12: Mea 5F 37
York Pl. LE67: Coal 1K 41
(off Stamford Dr.)
York Rd. DE11: Chu G 6J 21
York St. DE14: Bur T 3H 13
YOXALL 2B 16

Z

Zetland Cl. LE67: Coal 2D 40
Zion Hill LE67: Cole 1B 34

SAFETY CAMERA INFORMATION

PocketGPSWorld.com's CamerAlert is a self-contained speed and red light camera warning system for SatNavs and Android or Apple iOS smartphones/tablets. Visit www.cameralert.co.uk to download.

Safety camera locations are publicised by the Safer Roads Partnership which operates them in order to encourage drivers to comply with speed limits at these sites. It is the driver's absolute responsibility to be aware of and to adhere to speed limits at all times.

By showing this safety camera information it is the intention of Geographers' A-Z Map Company Ltd., to encourage safe driving and greater awareness of speed limits and vehicle speed. Data accurate at time of printing.